The LDS

ACTOR'S SCENEBOOK

Compiled and Edited by
C Michael Perry and Gayanne Ramsden
Introduction by *Agnes Broberg*
Volume 1

Salt Lake City

© 2013 by Zion BookWorks
ALL RIGHTS RESERVED

No portion of this book may be reproduced in any form without written permission from the publisher or the author's representative, except for brief passages quoted for review purposes.
Copyright and Permissions information for each individual play can be found in the back of this book.

First Edition(CS) – First Printing 2013
ISBN-13: 978-0615872063
ISBN-10: 0615872069
Kindle Edition: 2013
Trade Paperback Edition: 2013

Zion BookWorks
3877 Leicester Bay
South Jordan, UT 84095
*member of **LDSBA***

www.zionbookworks.com

Cover Layout by Bowen Design Works, Salt Lake City

Table of Contents

How this book is organized. All scenes and monologs are grouped together with the description of the play (in alphabetical order) that they have come from along with the pertinent character descriptions from that play. Each scene is introduced in its context as to what has happened previously. It is optimum that, when possible, you obtain a copy of the play and read it before performing the scene. Downloadable PDF files called PERUSAL FILES are available from the publisher in many cases. These files are free and often give much of the first half of the play, so you can get to know a little bit about the play and your characters. There are also several anthologies that contain the entire playscript of the plays you are interested in. These are available for purchase from different sources. A list is provided at the back of the book.

The scenes are listed here according to type and gender of the characters.

INTRODUCTION *i*

THOUGHTS on the Audition Itself *3*
THE TEN POINTS

THE SELECTIONS
MONOLOGS for Males
DRAMATIC MONOLOGUE: 1M(30-50)
  • *Cartwright (And Some Cried Fraud!)* *15*
DRAMATIC MONOLOGUE: 1M (40-60)
  • *David (The Anointed)* *19*
DRAMATIC MONOLOGUE: 1M(38)
  • *Joseph Smith (The Brothers)* *29*
SERIO-COMIC MONOLOGUE: 1M(30)
  • *Charlie Langly (Charlie's Monument)* *40*
SERIO-COMIC MONOLOGUE: 1M(teen)
  • *Brad (The Dance)* *54*
COMIC MONOLOGUE: 1M(30s)
  • *Howard (The Dance)* *56*
DRAMATIC MONOLOGUE: 1M(early 20s)
  • *Jack (Family)* *63*

DRAMATIC MONOLOGUE: 1M(30-50)
  • *Haight (Fire In The Bones)* — **71**
DRAMATIC MONOLOGUE: 1M(17)
  • *Helmuth (Huebener)* — **82**
DRAMATIC MONOLOGUE:1M(60)
  • *Robert M. Baines (Matters of the Heart)* — **103**
DRAMATIC MONOLOGUE:1M(35-50)
  • *Brigham Young (Move On!)* — **107**
COMIC MONOLOGUE:1M(25-40)
  • *Man 1 (Move On!)* — **109**
DRAMATIC MONOLOGUE:1M(35-50)
  • *Man 6 (Move On!)* — **110**
DRAMATIC MONOLOGUE:1M(30s)
  • *Boaz (The Plan)* — **115**
SERIO-COMIC MONOLOGUE: 1M (any age)
  • *Monologist (The Planemaker)* — **122**
DRAMATIC MONOLOGUE: 1M(teen)
  • *Billy (Reunion)* — **126**
DRAMATIC MONOLOGUE: 1M(30s)
  • *Wayne (Reunion)* — **127**
MONOLOGUE: 1M(30-50)
  • *Lamoni (A Sceptre, A Sword, A Scented Rose)* — **137**
MONOLOGUE: 1M(14)
  • *Jason (Teenage Witness to the Martyrdom)* — **158**

MONOLOGS for Females

SERIO-COMIC MONOLOGUE: 1W (30s)
  • *Alison (The Dance)* — **52**
DRAMATIC MONOLOGUE: 1W(late 20s)
  • *Deanna (Family)* — **62**
DRAMATIC MONOLOGUE: 1W (over 30)
  • *Pioneer Woman (The Forge and the Fire)* — **77**
DRAMATIC MONOLOGUE (with song): 1W(over 30)
  • *Contemporary Woman (The Forge and the Fire)* — **78**
SERIO-COMIC MONOLOGUE:1W(25-40)
  • *Irene (Move On!)* — **108**
DRAMATIC MONOLOGUE:1W(35-50)
  • *Woman 4 (Move On!)* — **111**
DRAMATIC MONOLOGUE:1W(20s)
  • *Ruth (The Plan)* — **113**
SERIO-COMIC MONOLOGUE: 1W (any age)
  • *Monologist (The Planemaker)* — **122**

DRAMATIC MONOLOGUE: 1W(over 30)
  • Abish (A Sceptre, A Sword, A Scented Rose)   **136**

SCENES for 1 Male and 1 Female
DRAMATIC SCENE: 1M(30-50) 1W(30-50)
  • Harper & Lewis (And Some Cried Fraud!)   **16**
DRAMATIC SCENE: 1M 1W
  • Saul(40s) Michal(18-22) (The Anointed)   **20**
DRAMATIC SCENE: 1M 1W (30s)
  • Joseph & Emma Act (The Brothers)   **30**
SERIO-COMIC SCENE: 1M(20s) 1W(20s)
  • Charlie & Nellie (Charlie's Monument)   **41**
DRAMATIC SCENE with SONG: 1M(boy of 10) 1W(30s)
  • Charlie & Faith (Charlie's Monument)   **46**
SERIO-COMIC SCENE: 1M(30s) 1F(girl of 4-9)
  • Charlie & Anna (Charlie's Monument)   **49**
DRAMATIC SCENE: 1M(50s) 1F(girl of 4-9)
  • Reeves & Anna   (Charlie's Monument)   **50**
SERIO-COMIC SCENE: 1M(18) 1W(23)
  • Brad & Janet (The Dance)   **57**
SERIO-COMIC SCENE: 1M 1W (30s)
  • Howard & Alison (The Dance)   **59**
DRAMATIC SCENE: 1M 1W (40s)
  • John D. Lee & Emma (Fire In The Bones)   **72**
COMIC SCENE: 1M 1W (20s)
  • Oliver & Martha (The Forge and the Fire)   **80**
SERIO-COMIC SCENE: 1M(30s) 1W(19-25)
  • Jedediah Grant & Susan Noble (Jedediah!)   **85**
DRAMATIC SCENE:1M 1W (late 50s)
  • Robert M. Baines & Alice Baines
    (Matters of the Heart)   **104**
DRAMATIC SCENE:1M 1W (16-22)
  • Lucifer, Gaia (The Plan)   **116**
DRAMATIC SCENE:1M 1W (19 & 26)
  • Jacob, Leah (The Plan)   **118**
DRAMATIC SCENE: 1M 1W (30s)
  • Chris & Wayne (Reunion)   **127**
DRAMATIC SCENE: 1M(late 20s) 1W (over 30)
  • Ammon & Abish
    (A Sceptre, A Sword, A Scented Rose)   **141**
DRAMATIC SCENE: 1M 1W (30s & 40-50)
  • SON (JESUS), MOTHER (MARY)

(Stones)	*154*
MUSICAL SCENE: 1M 1W (late 20s)	
• *Joseph Smith & Emma Smith*	
(They Called Him Brother Joseph)	*160*
DRAMATIC SCENE: 1M 1W (both teens)	
• *Penewah & Willkie (Wisdom Tree)*	*170*
DRAMATIC SCENE: 1M 1W (25-40)	
• *Venice & Denver (Wisdom Tree)*	*173*

SCENES for 2 Females

DRAMATIC SCENE: 2W (20s & 40s)	
• *Deanna & Mom (Family)*	*64*
DRAMATIC SCENE: 2W (over 30)	
• *Sephariah & Abish*	
(A Sceptre, A Sword, A Scented Rose)	*139*

SCENES for 2 Males

DRAMATIC SCENE: 2M (50-60 & 20s)	
• *Nathan, Solomon (The Anointed)*	*23*
DRAMATIC SCENE: 2M (20s)	
• *Firstborn & Bornfirst, Act One (Brothers)*	*25*
DRAMATIC SCENE: 2M (1boy, 1teen)	
• *Joseph Smith, Hyrum Smith (The Brothers)*	*33*
DRAMATIC SCENE: 2M (38 & 43)	
• *Joseph Smith, Hyrum Smith (The Brothers)*	*37*
DRAMATIC SCENE: 2M (over 40)	
• *John D. Lee & George Albert SMITH*	
(Fire In The Bones)	*73*
DRAMATIC SCENE: 2M(teens)	
• *Helmuth & Rudi (Huebener)*	*83*
DRAMATIC SCENE (with optional song): 2M (18-23 & 55-65)	
• *Alex MacRae & Sidney Rigdon (Liberty Jail)*	*87*
DRAMATIC SCENE (with optional songs): 2M (30s)	
• *Joseph Smith & Hyrum Smith (Liberty Jail)*	*90*
DRAMATIC SCENE (with optional song): 2M (30s)	
• *Joseph Smith & Lyman Wight (Liberty Jail)*	*95*
DRAMATIC SCENE: 2M (19 & 30s)	
• *Billy & Wayne (Reunion)*	*133*
DRAMATIC SCENE: 2M (25-30 & over 35)	
• *Ammon & Lamoni*	*145*
(A Sceptre, A Sword, A Scented Rose)	
DRAMATIC SCENE: 2M (over 35)	

    • *Jakor & Lamoni*
(A Sceptre, A Sword, A Scented Rose)   ***148***
DRAMATIC SCENE: 2M (40-70 & 16-30)
    • *FATHER (ABRAHAM), SON (ISAAC)*
    (Stones)   ***150***
MUSICAL SCENE: 2M(1teen & 20s)
    • *Joseph Smith & Alvin Smith*
    (They Called Him Brother Joseph)   ***163***
COMIC SCENE: 2M
    • *Brian & Matt (mid-20s)*
    (The Unfortunate Courtship of Brian Tanner)   ***167***
SERIO-COMIC SCENE (optional song): 2M (11-12 & 30s)
    • *Matt & Jay (Wisdom Tree)*   ***175***

SCENE for 1 Male and 2 Females
DRAMATIC SCENE: 1M 2W (younger than 25)
    • *Calvin, Marilyn & Linda*
    (Martyr In Waiting)   ***100***

LIST of copyrights and permissions   *178*
RESOURCES   *181*

Zion BookWorks

INTRODUCTION

One of the most difficult tasks facing a theatre educator is finding appropriate material for students to use in practice sessions and for performance. Whether the student is preparing a class performance or for competition the search for material is a rigorous task. Students are often left to find their own resources.

In today's society most students and many new and/or over-worked teachers search the Internet for material. Unfortunately the majority of dramatic literature available on the Internet is highly unsuitable for students of any age. I have had students perform pieces gleaned from Internet sources that made me uncomfortable. They are also not very dramatically worthy.

Suitability of performance material is doubly important in communities with high moral standards. A community where students display positive morality and parents expect schools to support the ethics of society requires theatre educators to choose and introduce students to literature that is uplifting.

This new compilation of performance material by C. Michael Perry, brings to students and busy teachers a marvelous new resource of Latter-day Saint works. There are not only selections that fulfill curriculum requirements but also ones that can inspire student performers who want to present works that support their beliefs. In addition parents need not worry about what their child is performing in the theatre classroom.

Not only do the monologues and scenes represent LDS topics but they are well-written and dramatically worthy. Among the works are pieces taken from some of the best and most beloved LDS authors. Students who choose to perform from this new collection will be challenged. But they will never feel uncomfortable.

Congratulations to Michael for creating such a usable and positive collection!

In addition I was very impressed by the special AUDITION section of the book. When student actors approach an audition so many of them have little or no experience and often attend auditions totally unprepared. Oh, they are memorized and ready to perform but they have no concept of what else is entailed in the audition process.

Mr. Perry goes through the auditioning process clearly and succinctly. Besides understanding the concrete aspects of auditioning, it's easy for a beginner to grasp the finesse needed to complete a successful audition. If a beginning actor follows the information contained in audition section he will feel much more comfortable and prepared to excel at his audition.

Agnes Broberg

THOUGHTS ON THE AUDITION ITSELF

Why do we audition? Hasn't anyone figured out a better system? The simple answer is "No!"

The purpose of an audition is not to get the part, it is not to get cast -- it is to be called back for the Final Auditions or Callbacks. So what do you have to do to get a callback? Get noticed. And not in an annoying way that makes the Auditior's eyes roll, or eyebrows raise, or head shake in the "Why me?" mode; which emotional state is inevitably followed by the utterance of a too early, "Next!" from the person who was supposed to be looking at you, noticing you.

You want them to look at you *because* you seem to know what you are doing on stage. You are comfortable there. Not that you won't be nervous. Everyone gets nervous. And they understand that! Believe me, they do. But what they must be able to do is sense something in you that will be useful to them in creating this piece of theatre. You want to do something, or say something in such a way that it forces them to look up from their script for a minute, something that diverts them from the little discussion they are having because they are not listening to you; nor did they listen to the last person who did not make them sit up and take notice of what they were doing or saying.

Many people do interviews as well as talent auditions. It helps the auditor get to know who might be the best personality fit for the company of actors that the Director/Auditor is trying to put together.

One thing you CANNOT do during this interview is 'act.' You must be yourself. Certainly be your best self, but if you are positive, cocky, self-assured, even a little egotistical, let that come out. All these qualities are a part of a good actor -- the best and the worst. The Director/Auditor is just trying to balance and gauge how you will fit into the company -- maybe even *if* you will fit in. You don't know what he/she is looking for, so why try to guess? You might guess wrongly. Always be yourself, warts and all. But maybe the warts could use a little filing down, or even some Compound W!

SO -- HOW DO WE GET NOTICED?

I'll tell you in Ten Points.
- Be fresh.
- Be alert.
- Dress in something memorable, but not provocative. (And wear the same thing to the callback, when you get one.)
- Know your material.
- Know your character (inside and out).
- If singing is a part of the audition, know your song cold. Work on it.
- If it is a dance audition, wear clothes that you can move in.
- If it is a cold reading, know the story before you go in. (If it is an original, that may be difficult, but know something about the show. Research it.)
- Be flexible. (Be willing to take direction, whether it agrees with your concept and research or not!)
- Let them see a technique, some technique, any technique -- even if you only know one, use it! -- not just raw talent.

(More on all this later.)

Can anyone be an actor? You've heard it a thousand times that some famous actor didn't even audition; they were seen along the side of the road and called in, sometimes to an audition for a role which they eventually landed, but usually just to be cast in the role. This does happen, but don't count on it. The answer, again, is 'No! Not everyone can be an actor.' Many people possess the basic qualities to being a good actor: an open mind and a closed mouth! Those who do not possess these qualities may find themselves left out. A Director or Casting Agent wants listeners and doers, not someone who knows it all and is ready to demonstrate their knowledge verbally on the turn of every page, or even in between sentences.

When you do not get cast -- and it will be a when, not an if -- do not feel like you failed. There are many reasons that a person is not cast in a show, or even called back. Most of them have nothing to do with talent. The look, the physicality, is a big factor. Maybe THE biggest factor. Age, size, weight, build, frame, hair color (less so, but still a factor), the way you walk, sit, stand, dance -- even your speech patterns, accents and regionalisms -- these are all things that will 'disqualify' or 'qualify' you for a role. And remember there is nothing wrong with you physically. It is just that the Director or Casting Agent does not see you in that role. Can you change their perceptions? Sometimes -- if you really get them to see you 'newly'. But what they see is rarely within your control. So don't sweat it. There is always another audition!

NOW, TO ELABORATE ON *THE TEN POINTS*.

Point One
Be fresh.

Change your material from time to time. Add new material often. Have more than one monologue prepared. Serious, comic, serio-comic, contemporary, classical, avante-garde, at least two of each. They do not need to be long for audition purposes -- no more than a minute, usually. As a matter of fact, use your drama class and workshop experiences to build your audition portfolio. When you get a callback the auditors will often ask you if you have anything else prepared. When you say you do, and pull out something as impressive as your first audition piece, they will know that you are serious about what you do. They will 'notice' you! It could get you another callback or even the role.

This applies to audition songs as well. Make sure that you have a representative of styles (ballad, up-tempo, showstoppers) and composers. (If you use Sondheim, be sure to also have Rodgers and Hammerstein, Lerner & Loewe, Rodgers and Hart, Porter, Herman, Kander and Ebb, Loesser, and Jason Robert Brown, others.)

Don't choose the same material that other people are using to excess just because it is the popular song at the moment. I can't count the times that I, as an auditor, have heard upwards of 20 people perform "Bring Him Home" or "On My Own" from LES MIZ in ONE audition session. Avoid certain songs like the plague. Your auditors want to hear something they haven't heard. It makes you more memorable; especially if you perform it well! Choose great songs from lesser known musicals. Make sure that your songs fit the show you are auditioning for. The same can be said for monologues. Avoid Shakespeare unless you are auditioning for a company that does Shakespeare. And if you do Shakespeare, choose the shorter, lesser known pieces from anything but 'Hamlet' or 'R&J', unless you are auditioning for those plays.

Point Two
Be alert.

Get your rest, eat well, warm up your body, your voice -- and your mind -- before entering that audition room. The life of an actor is often a harried one. Try to mitigate that through proper sleep habits. We theatre people are night creatures, that is true. But if you have an audition at 9 AM, get to bed early. Sure, the show you are in may have ended at 11 PM the previous night, but if you really want a chance at the audition tomorrow -- SLEEP. Don't go out with your friends and party.

Don't eat a lot before an audition, especially if you are the nervous, stomach-churning type of auditioner, but eat something -- and make it healthy. No Pop Tarts! An egg and toast, with a little juice will suffice. Yogurt and fruit. But watch the dairy products if you are going to sing. And no pop at all before an audition! (Or a performance, for that matter!)

Get into a routine every day, if not only before performances and auditions. Go through the physical regimen of attuning yourself to your body each day, relaxing your muscles. Singer or actor or both -- use gentle warm-up exercises to wake-up your voice every day! What warms up your mind? Contemplation -- even 15 minutes of it will help focus you. The traditional Constructive Rest position is a great one to accomplish the mind and body warm-up. But to keep your mind sharp and attuned, read something -- anything -- fiction or non-fiction, or even a play. Especially the play you are auditioning for. If you know something about it, it will come out in your audition.

Point Three
Dress in something memorable, but not provocative. (And wear the same thing to the callback, when you get one.)

Not much more to say here, except that you can dress for the role, if you desire. Dress to the age and the idiosyncrasies of whomever it is that you are auditioning to be. But only go close to the character, because if you guess wrong, the auditors will see that and not see *you* in the role. Dress young, dress old, dress frumpy. If your character is a business person, wear a suit or look like a business person. (But then bring clothes to dance in. See Point Seven.)

Point Four

Know your material.

Do your homework, your research. Don't just pick a monlogue because it sounds fun or because you saw someone else do it, and liked it. That is only a starting point. Make it yours! Read the play, the novel, see the movie! Even the Cliff's Notes on the title would be helpful.

Know something about the author and his other works. Know something about the period that the play is set in, both the audition piece you've selected and the play you're auditioning for. Be prepared.

If it is a cold reading, all of the same research applies -- only double. The more you know about the play, its author and time-period, the closer you will be to nailing the audition.

Point Five

Know your character (inside and out).

Know what your character likes, whom or what it is in the play that they do NOT like. Make up little things that seem to go along with the character as presented in the source material. Favorite food, activity, color, author, vacation they may have taken or long to take. It is the little things that build a performance -- and you are *performing* for the auditors. Give it everything within your power and talent to help you come off at the top of the list.

If it is a cold reading, ask the right questions to get a sense of the character, but not too many. Ask ONE pertinent question that you feel will give you the most information. Then be sure to use what you learned from that question in the reading you will give. Then, let the director direct you if he/she chooses to.

Point Six

If singing is a part of the audition, know your song

cold. Work on it.

Never, ever, ever, ever, sing a song you are not totally familiar with. Do not choose a song the day before you are to audition and think you can 'wing it'! It is better to do a song you know (and maybe that the auditors have heard too many times) than to risk a new song that is untried. Bring the sheet music for the pianist (or an accompanist of your own) AND an accompaniment track on a CD or mp3. If the pianist is not there, you're on anyway!

Point Seven

If it is a dance audition, wear clothes that you can move in.

Ladies -- no heels unless they are on character shoes. Men -- avoid muscle types of shirts if there is no muscle. Like a ballet class the auditors want to see not just how you can dance, but how your body moves. Don't wear clothes that show off every line and feature of your body, like leotards and tights, unless you are comfortable with that. If you are a trained dancer, that might be the best thing to wear, since it is what you are used to. A loose fitting slack and a t-shirt might be the best things over all. Wear clothes that allow you to move. Avoid sweat clothes of any kind. They cover up too much and they are loose, which can bind your movements. Jeans are hard to dance in because they do not stretch. Solid shoes -- the best is a character or jazz shoe for men or women. They are made for the theatre. It is another sign to the auditors that you have some kind of experience.

Point Eight

If it is a cold reading, know the story before you go in. (If it is an original, that may be difficult, but know something about the show. Research it.)

If you can get a hold of the copy of a play, do so and read it! If it is a musical, listen to the score, Most libraries are great sources to get a hold of a script or a CD.

If an agency is casting a show they will often have a script at the agency that you can go in and read. Also with the internet, many theatres post audition materials on their websites.

If you cannot get a hold of the play, and it is based on a novel or short story, or film, read it or see it! (Again think local library.) Do your homework! This is your livelihood we are talking about. Your passion. Even if you are amateur in status, you can 'act' like a professional.

Point Nine
Be flexible.

This does not necessarily refer to your dancer's body. Many people can dance well enough without being terribly flexible.

Auditions are a tedious thing for the auditors and for those being auditioned. They may run long, someone ahead of you may not show up and you may have to perform before you expected to. Always arrive early by at least a half an hour for an audition and be prepared to stay at least a half an hour longer than your schedule. If it is a Cattle Call, just be there early and prepare to stay late.

But be willing to take direction, whether it agrees with your concept and research or not! So what if Hamlet's Mother is not a coquette. If the Director asks you to play it that way -- give it everything you've got!

Don't be surprised if they talk to you about things that have nothing to do with acting. The Interview is a subtle signal that they are interested in you. Always have something ready to say about your life and hopes and dreams -- even your family. Keep it short and simple, they do not need your life's history. Just a few interesting, pertinent, funny or even sad morsels tossed their way will pique their interest.

Point Ten
Let them see a technique, some technique, any technique -- even if you only know one, use it! -- not just raw talent.

Whether you've studied Stanislavski, Boleslavsky, Meisner, Adler, or any of the other acting systems out there, choose several points, from any one or all, that you feel would be best to take with you into your cold reading audition. Some of

Michael Shurtleff's Twelve Guideposts would be smashingly helpful. I have found the Shurtleff guidepost called 'Opposites' to be particularly useful when auditioning. His 'Relationships' guide is also helpful. It's kind of like a Stanislavski 'What If?'. If you are given the time at the cold audition to prepare, then I have found that the traditional, "Objective, Obstacle, Tactic" is also of great assistance.

Stay away from Stanislavski's 'Emotional Memory' at an audition. It can do you in! It is a rehearsal technique only.

If you have prepared something for an audition, then use every technique with which you feel comfortable. If you have a friend who can help you, perform for them. An acting coach is a great audience. Just don't perform for someone who is also auditioning. You don't want to give away all your secrets.

But be sure to observe Point Nine!

Nothing will ever guarantee a call back or being cast in a certain coveted role. Acting is a business AND a craft. We are so fortunate to be allowed to ply our craft while earning a living, or while pursuing a passion. For the professional or the amateur, they both proceed out of a love for what we are doing.

Study. Learn. Practice. Study again. Practice some more. And Learn all over again.

With every audition or role the process is repeated. And every audition or role is unique and a whole new experience. The only thing that is the same is the process: Study. Learn. Practice.

Break A Leg!

Zion BookWorks

The Selections

Zion BookWorks

The LDS ACTOR'S Scenebook -- Volume 1

And Some Cried Fraud!
A Play by *Thom Duncan*

ABOUT THE PLAY: This play is a fantasy. It sets the Book of Mormon in a courtroom with a Judge, Prosecuting Attorney, Defense Attorney and witnesses for the defense and the prosecution. The jury is the audience. But the arguments presented are heated and divisive. David Whitmer, Martin Harris, Oliver Cowdery and Charles Anthon, and others, are cross-examined and the Book is upheld as truth.

DRAMATIC MONOLOGUE: 1M or 1W • Cartwright, Act Two
ABOUT THE CHARACTER:
HAL CARTWRIGHT: A proponent and defender of The Church, The Book of Mormon and all things pertaining to God. (Could be played by a Woman)

CARTWRIGHT: And I agree with you. All these things are possible. Now, bear with me for a minute as I share with you something from the writings of Ixtlilxochitl, and see what the answer to the question "Could Joseph Smith have known this?" will be when I'm finished. I quote: "And before going on, I want to make an account of Natzin, the astrologer... Before dying, he gathered together all the histories the Toltecas had, from the creation of that world up to this time, and had them pictured in a very large book--" Funny he should say, "Pictured in a very large book." Sounds like he's talking about some language like Egyptian or something. Again I quote: "--where were pictured all the persecutions and hardships, properties and good happenings, kings and lords, laws and good government of their ancestors, old sayings and good examples, temples, idols, sacrifices, rites and ceremonies that they had, astrology, philosophy, architecture, and the other arts, good as well as bad, and a resumé of all things of science, knowledge, prosperous and adverse battles, and many things; and he entitled his book calling it Teomoxtli, which well interpreted means the Various Things of God and Divine Book; the natives now call the Holy Scriptures Teomoztli, because it is almost the same, principally in the persecutions and hardships of men."

DRAMATIC SCENE: 1M 1W • Harper & Lewis Act One
ABOUT THE CHARACTERS:
JAMES HARPER: counsel for the prosecution who seems to be a hater. There is something inside him that rises up at religious things. What tragic accident or happening could have taken place in his past to make him so bitter? And what is said during the trial that touches that sore spot.
JESSICA LEWIS: A scientist and a defender of the Faith.

(LEWIS *is in a chair.* HARPER *stands. A pause. He looks toward the spot where the other lawyer,* CARTWRIGHT, *sits.*)
HARPER: Dr. Lewis....
LEWIS: *(A bit nervously.)* Yes?
HARPER: I found that scripture reference in Ezekiel quite interesting.
LEWIS: Most people do. When they understand what it means.
HARPER: It's quite obvious that someday, there will be two books of equal scriptural value. If I might, I'd like to refer to that scripture again.
(Takes Bible)
Ezekiel 37, 15 through 17, wasn't it? Ah, here we are. Here's the part I'm interested in. "The Work of the Lord came unto me, saying etc., etc."
LEWIS: Yes. God talking to Ezekiel.
HARPER: Exactly. And God, several lines later, still speaking to Ezekiel, tells him to write the Book of Joseph. "Take another stick and write upon it, for Joseph, etc." Dr. Lewis, did Ezekiel write the Book of Mormon?
LEWIS: No...
HARPER: Then the Book of Mormon cannot be the book to

which Ezekiel is referring, because he was commanded to write it.
LEWIS: But you'll remember he was commanded to write the Book of Judah, also. He didn't write all of it. I believe this scripture is not as specific as you maintain. When God said, "Thou son of man," he wasn't speaking to just Ezekiel, but to other prophets as well.
HARPER: That may be so. But it doesn't say that, does it?
LEWIS: Not in those--actual words, no.
HARPER: In "actual" words, what does it say? Who is God "actually" commanding to write the Stick of Joseph?
LEWIS: Ezekiel, but....
HARPER: Let's suppose, just to let you know I'm not close-minded, let's assume you are correct. Why couldn't Joseph Smith have one day been reading the Book of Ezekiel and--lo and behold'--look what he finds! Another book of Scripture is needed! he says to himself. He writes it, and when people ask him why isn't it mentioned in the Bible? he says, "Oh, but it is! Right here in Ezekiel! "Now couldn't that have been the way the Book of Mormon fulfills this prophecy?
LEWIS: No.
HARPER: You say no. Why?
LEWIS: Because it didn't happen that way.
HARPER: How do you know?
LEWIS: Well, I don't--really....
HARPER: Then it could have happened that way, couldn't it have?
LEWIS: I don't believe that it did.
HARPER: I'm not asking you what you believe. I'm asking if you can offer any evidence to prove what I have just said did not take place.
LEWIS: No. I can't.
HARPER: Thank you.
   (a pause)
You said the Bible makes mention of other books?
   (No answer.)
Dr. Lewis?
LEWIS: *(Somewhat intimidated by HARPER now.)* Y--yes?
HARPER: I asked you a question.
LEWIS: I'm sorry.
HARPER: That's all right. I'll ask it again. You said the Bible

makes mention of other books?

LEWIS: Yes.

HARPER: In fact, you name some of them: Book of the Covenant, etc.

LEWIS: There are also the Lost Epistles of Paul.

HARPER: I'm sure there are. Now, if what the Mormons believe is true, that the Book of Mormon is the second most important book ever written, why is it merely alluded to, while all these other books get front page treatment?

LEWIS: I couldn't say.

HARPER: Doesn't that seem strange to you? That God so misplaced his priorities? Going to all that trouble to name these secondary works while giving only an honorable mention to the Book of Mormon?

LEWIS: I would hesitate to second-guess God.

HARPER: What if God, while He was rattling off these other works, had slipped in the title, the Book of Mormon? Wouldn't that have made it a lot easier? Then we wouldn't even need this trial.

LEWIS: Yes, we would. Because someone would have just claimed that Joseph Smith stole the title.

HARPER: You're right, Dr. Lewis. That wouldn't prove anything, would it? And your interpretation of that passage in Ezekiel doesn't prove anything either, does it?

The Anointed
A Musical Play by *Thomas F. Rogers*
and C. Michael Perry

ABOUT THE PLAY: THE ANOINTED is unusual in its construction. It harkens more to the classical Greek form than anything modern. The words and thoughts are poetic. There is even a type of Greek Chorus present. But the story of the epic struggle the Lord had to get a temple built in Jerusalem, through weak men, is moving and solid. The dialogue scenes are full of imagery; like a passage from the Bible happening in front of our eyes. The central character, of course, is David. Beginning with so much promise and ending so ignominiously, his story is the pattern of pride that could bring the downfall of every man.

<u>DRAMATIC MONOLOGUE: 1M • *David, Act Two*</u>
ABOUT THE CHARACTER:
DAVID: Was the "Golden Boy", had more promise than any other in the Bible. Because much was given, much was expected -- and so much was lost; not to God, but to David and his people. Pride, envy, lust -- they all besieged David and proved his ruin. Fear entered his life as he began sinning against the Lord, and each sin covered up (from all but the Lord) brought his downfall even lower and caused him more fear.

> *The scene is DAVID's Court. He has just told his son, Solomon, to kill JOAB. SOLOMON has questioned why it should be so.* (Stricken line)

~~SOLOMON: But why must he die after all this time... so many years...?~~

DAVID: Why...? Why...? There are many reasons: He is no longer useful to me now that I am no longer king... and as an example, for your future protection...*and* I must abide by my oath, be true to my word. Otherwise, I would not be just... No, it will be good to be rid of cousin Joab--Joab, who always meddled. Oh, he was a great statesman, most reliable, most conscientious, but he always meddled in my affairs... All but one: and there he didn't meddle enough--which has always made me wonder. Why didn't he take more care for Absalom...? No, without Joab, I can think my own thoughts again--not a King's thoughts maybe, but David's. That is all right, isn't it? Since I am no longer King...? Show constant friendship to the family of Barzillai of Gilead: let them have their place at your table; they befriended me when I was a fugitive from Absalom. And do not forget Shimei son of Gera, the Benjamite from Bahurim, who cursed me bitterly the day I fled to Mahanaim. True, he came down to meet me at the Jordan, and I swore by the Lord that I would not put him to death. Bring down his grey hairs in blood to the grave also. Guiltless and blessed be the Lord's anointed!

DRAMATIC SCENE: 1M 1W • Saul, Michal, Act One
ABOUT THE CHARACTERS:
SAUL: *Anointed King of Israel by Samuel, given the rights, privileges and powers that God wanted a King to have only to trample them under his feet. Saul was supposed to be a miracle. He began well but ended in shame. Distrustful, proud, afraid, he enlists others to carry out what he cannot.*
MICHAL: *his dutiful and beautiful daughter. She is not what you might think of as a righteous woman. She is young and inexperienced, but loves her father and is fascinated by this strange shepherd boy that she and her brother Jonathan have 'grown up' with. She is loyal. But to whom? She has grown to love David. But why?*

> *This scene begins the play and is the throne room. SAUL is seated. Michal enters.)*

MICHAL: Father?
SAUL: Sit.
(She does so.)
SAUL: I wish to speak to you of your future.
MICHAL: And David's?

SAUL: *(laughing)* No, and not David's. I wish you no early grave.
MICHAL: Father?
SAUL: Your future will be carefree.
MICHAL: But David?
SAUL: <u>Without</u> David.
MICHAL: David is dead, Father?
SAUL: He will not survive this campaign. He was outnumbered ten to one, I saw to that. Ten Philistines to one Israelite, and he knew it. But he still took the bait, the boaster. Still vowed to lead the charge.
MICHAL: Bait?
SAUL: Your hand, of course. Why else would I betroth you?
MICHAL: Sire. Am I only a plaything?!
SAUL: I could not tell you sooner. You'd have lacked heart and failed to entice him.
MICHAL: But why do you hate David? He was always loyal and has served you well. Have you forgotten which Bethlehemite slew Goliath?
SAUL: I remember all too well.
MICHAL: And his many victories against the Philistines?
SAUL: Indeed! "Saul has slain his thousands," they sang.
MICHAL: He slew them for you. He did not wish to be your rival.
SAUL: Are you so sure? Is it not rumored that as a child he was anointed to succeed me?
MICHAL: He never said so himself.
SAUL: He was too clever for that, just as he at first pretended not to desire you as his wife. Don't I, once a lowly Benjamite, understand his kind of cunning--and the people's childish ways? They rejected old Samuel.
MICHAL: The prophet?
SAUL: They wanted no more Abrahams or Moseses. They sought praise, not condemnation. They sought to be like our enemies, with a King to lead them to war and fight their battles.
MICHAL: So Samuel's sons could not succeed him?
SAUL: *(laughing)* Samuel still had the last word. He chose the lowliest Israelite from the smallest and poorest of all twelve tribes.
MICHAL: Samuel or the Lord?

SAUL: Who can say? Besides, did I not seek out Samuel myself.

MICHAL: Did you know then that the Lord had told his prophet to anoint the first Benjamite who would come to him? And did it all happen--as Samuel had predicted?

SAUL: All? Yes, all.

MICHAL: Then it was surely of the Lord, not Samuel...

SAUL: It would seem so, wouldn't it? It was long ago. But I must have had an intimation. Else why would I have gone so out of my way?

MICHAL: Perhaps the Lord led you. They say that Israel's first young king was mighty in battle because the Lord was with him.

SAUL: They say... yes, they say. But if the Lord was with me, why did he never tell me to build a temple?

MICHAL: A temple?

MICHAL: But if the Lord was really not with you, what is said of David may yet be.

SAUL: Exactly. If he was not anointed, how did he alone of all Israel, a young unhardened warrior fresh from Bethlehem, dare defy Goliath? His first day in camp and he, embarrassing his brothers, called out, more than once "What shall be done?" It's already legend. Proverbial. Israel's mothers put their children to bed with the telling of it. Perhaps you are right though. Perhaps he didn't mean to be my rival. But he might have become such, even against his will. Had he lived on, the people would have preferred him. And he'd have had no choice but to depose me.

MICHAL: Do <u>you</u> fear David?

SAUL: I have feared not David but his reputation, and with each passing victory I have had more reason. But I fear no longer. He will not return.

MICHAL: Though God may favor him?

SAUL: Not this time. And as for you--we must discuss new suitors.

MICHAL: *(to herself)* Oh father! What you don't put me through: First you command me to slink and sway before a ruddy shepherd boy -- his knees and elbows scabbed and scuffed -- his garments coarse and worn -- a boy with matted hair and tongue as thick with graceless speech. You make me smile at him and fold him in my arms. And when he's

scrubbed and combed and learns the proper phrases, his natural strength and candor overcomes me. Father! What you don't put me through. Please father, let us at least wait until the messengers return from battle that my mourning may not lack heart, for I did love him. And perchance... perchance--
SAUL: Chance will not help you. I have seen to that, and even if it should, he will never meet the condition of your marriage.
MICHAL: The foreskins?
SAUL: He will never harvest ten or twenty let alone the hundred he agreed to. Sooner would the Philistine claim his, though his is long absent.
MICHAL: *(fingering a wall-hung lyre)* Will his song never more content you?
SAUL: No song will ever content me as did his, but all the same I will rest easier.

DRAMATIC SCENE: 2M • Nathan, Solomon, Act Two
ABOUT THE CHARACTERS:
NATHAN: God's Prophet, after Samuel. He has waited long to deliver this message to build a Temple. He has seen so much failure in the men who have risen to Kingship in Israel. He hopes that Solomon will be the one.
SOLOMON: David's son, David's promise, David's blessing. Imperfect, but steadfast -- to a point. He has the desire to be great. He has infinite wisdom. He has great wealth and the trust of the Lord. For now.

(I include this scene because of its poetry and its construction in large speeches. The Throne room again.)
NATHAN (AS JEHOVAH): What shall I give thee? Tell me...
SOLOMON: Thou didst nonetheless show great and constant love to Thy Servant David my father, because <u>before</u> Thee, if not before other men, he ever walked in loyalty, righteousness and integrity of heart. Thou hast maintained Thy great and constant love towards him by granting him a

son to succeed him on the throne. Now, O Lord my God, Thou hast made Thy Servant King in place of my father David, though I am a mere child, unskilled in leadership. And I am here in the midst of Thy people, the people of Thy choice, too many to be numbered or counted. Therefore give Thy Servant a heart with skill to listen, to govern Thy people justly and distinguish good from evil. For who is equal to the task of governing this Thy great people?

NATHAN (AS JEHOVAH): Because thou hast asked for this, and not for long life or for wealth, or for the lives of thine enemies, but hast asked for discernment in administering justice, I grant thy request: I give thee a heart so wise and so understanding that there has been none like thee before thy time nor will be after thee. This much I can give thee. The Spirit of what I give--which one day men will call fellow feeling, empathy, compassion, forgiveness, mercy, grace--will bestow upon all men at the meridian of time with my own coming....I give thee furthermore those things for which thou didst not ask--wealth and honor no King can match. And if thou dost conform to my ways and observe my ordinances and commandments...I will give thee long life... and David, through thee, a divine descendant!

CHORUS: A divine descendant!

SOLOMON: Allow... allow me, if it be Thy will, to build Thee a house in Thy name-

NATHAN (AS JEHOVAH): Thou, Solomon, if thou art righteous, shalt also build my temple.

SOLOMON: *(shouting)* Power and glory be unto Thee forever, worlds without end!!

Brothers
A Play by *J. Scott Bronson*

ABOUT THE PLAY; The play is a discussion between the FIRST brothers -- Lucifer and Jehovah. They discuss their missions (funny term), their hopes, their philosophies -- their Father. It is an exploration of what it means to be a brother, to have a potential and a promise -- or not. There is a universality present, founded in the beginnings of time, that resonates throughout all time and beyond; speaks to all brothers everywhere.

DRAMATIC SCENE: 2M • *Firstborn & Bornfirst, Act One*
ABOUT THE CHARACTERS:
FIRSTBORN -- *the one who is foreordained to great Joy*
BORNFIRST -- *the one who would not be able to fulfill the Joy he chose for others*

(They are in a Pre-Existence. Even before the Great Council. BORNFIRST draws near to his brother, a hopeful expression inviting complicity.)

FIRSTBORN: When is it, then, that you think Father should offer the choice to surrender my will?

BORNFIRST: Now. Before we go into the world.

(FIRSTBORN is bewildered for a moment.)

FIRSTBORN: But, that changes the entire plan ... completely.

BORNFIRST: Yes!

FIRSTBORN: The whole point of the plan is to see what we will choose ... in the world.

BORNFIRST: No. No ... I disagree. The point of the plan is to find out what we really want.

FIRSTBORN: ... Yes.

BORNFIRST: And we all want to come home.

FIRSTBORN: ... Yes.

BORNFIRST: So, let's choose it now.

FIRSTBORN: But that proves nothing.

BORNFIRST: It proves our love and devotion to Father—
FIRSTBORN: But it will mean nothing.
BORNFIRST: *(In a sudden and fleeting rage)* It will mean everything to us.
 (Pause.)
FIRSTBORN: How?
BORNFIRST: Imagine the reward.
FIRSTBORN: I <u>know</u> the reward.
BORNFIRST: If that were true, then you would understand what it is that I'm trying to share with you. You would reach out with me and take hold of what is waiting out there for us.
FIRSTBORN: What is that?
BORNFIRST: Glory.
 (Pause.)
FIRSTBORN: Brother, we can not take that glory upon us. It can only be given. Wait—. Let me speak. You <u>know</u> that I am right. I know that you know. You are deceiving yourself. And you may end up deceiving many others. You are greatly admired. We all look up to you. Please do not do this.
 (Pause.)
BORNFIRST: You are the one who is deceived, little brother. Though we came to this stage of life at nearly the same moment, the fact that I preceded you seems now to hold a compelling significance.
FIRSTBORN: Is that so?
BORNFIRST: Oh yes.
 (Pause.)
 You are weak. You haven't the strength of intellect or will to see that Father wants us to take his place as the saviors of his children. You, as the father of all living. And me as the redeemer of their souls.
FIRSTBORN: What's to redeem if their wills are not their own?
BORNFIRST: True. That will render the atonement a mere formality. But it will be necessary for them to see so that they will know to whom they must offer their obeisance—

FIRSTBORN: Father—
BORNFIRST: Me!
FIRSTBORN: You.
BORNFIRST: Me. I am, after all, the Firstborn of the father.
FIRSTBORN: You were born first, yes. But, Firstborn is a title. It must be earned. Like Father's glory, it must be given. You can not take it upon you.
BORNFIRST: Wrong, Brother. I will take it. Because it is mine.
FIRSTBORN: Wrong. It is Father's to give. To whom he will.
 (Pause.)
BORNFIRST: If not to me, then who?
FIRSTBORN: To whom he will.
BORNFIRST: To you? Is that what you think? You imagine that you can take my place?
FIRSTBORN: No. Of course not. Your place can not be taken. Only given.
BORNFIRST: To you?
FIRSTBORN: To whom Father will.
 (Pause.)
BORNFIRST: I will fight you.
FIRSTBORN: There is no need for that.
BORNFIRST: Oh, but there is. I will not let anyone—you or Father—take from me what is rightfully mine.
FIRSTBORN: If you pursue this course, it will not be taken, you will be giving it away.
BORNFIRST: *(Laughing)* Oh, yes. I was right. You are clever with words, aren't you?
FIRSTBORN: Call it clever if you like. I merely speak the truth.
BORNFIRST: Brother, you need to learn the difference between what is actually true, and what you merely believe to be true.
FIRSTBORN: Then teach me, Brother. What is the difference?
 (Pause.)
 You have no answer?

BORNFIRST: The difference is in what I believe to be true.

FIRSTBORN: Brother, I beg you, please do not follow this dangerous course.

BORNFIRST: Better that you should beg me for mercy.
   (Pause.)

FIRSTBORN: Well. A threat, is it.

BORNFIRST: A promise.

FIRSTBORN: Tell me.

BORNFIRST: That if you do not follow me in this course—this course that you call dangerous, but that I know to be true—when the time comes—when the world has been rolled up and given to Father for judgement, you will find yourself unworthy. On the outside of the law.
   (Beat.)
And you will no longer be my brother.
   (Pause.)

FIRSTBORN: My brother. All of this will be true. But you are the one who will be outside of the law. You are the one who will be the enemy of heaven.
   (Beat.)
But, you will always be my brother.
   (Pause.)

BORNFIRST: The Firstborn of Father's children.

FIRSTBORN: No. Born first.
   (Blackout.)

The Brothers
A Play by *Christie Lund Coles*

ABOUT THE PLAY: THE BROTHERS *bites off a lot of time and history but manages to chew it up thoughtfully and put on display the inner motions of this Boy Prophet and his older brother: Joseph and Hyrum Smith at different periods throughout their all-too-short lives. The times in which they lived, the challenges they faced, the inseparable nature of their loyalty to each other all lead to the inevitable conclusion -- their martyrdom. They were up to the task. They could do what God asked of them. And they did do it, willingly.*

DRAMATIC MONOLOGUE: 1M • Joseph Act Two Scene 3
ABOUT THE CHARACTER:
JOSEPH: *Joseph Smith, the Prophet of the restoration, is in his late thirties. He knows the end; he knows it will come soon, but not how soon.*

> *The Mansion House. JOSEPH is alone in the room. He begins from stillness, hands clasped behind his back.*

JOSEPH: The light grows dim, the wick is burning low. My heart is desolate beyond relief of tears. So like a light that has flamed clear and true in white intensity, my life that now seems void. And lonely as the wind that howls the night rapping the windows and my very soul with it's dark desolation. Oh, my Father whose very voice has spoken to my soul, whose pristine presence has appeared to me ... a boy, not different than other boys have been, yet more intense, perhaps, wanting to know, destined somehow, to run this chosen path. Difficult, most hazardous to the soul, and blessed ... and almost cursed ... I think, to know truths that the purest of angels gave to me, why must I stand here now, alone, entombed within the darkness of my pain, my loss? Have you forsaken me, removed your arm that has sustained me?

I must not think so blasphemously.

> *(He drops to his knees)*

Forgive me Father, and give me strength to bear all things that come, all loss, all grief. There have been many hours even as now, when to deny the things these mortal eyes have seen and marveled on, would have been easy, would have been the way to peace of mind, to rest, to a surcease of the torment of the crowd, to the jeers of those who saw and mocked me; the accusations of even those who should be dear ... Now, even the elect have turned aside. Sidney and Oliver, of the chosen few who held within their hands the promised book; hefted it, touched its gleaming plates, and swore that they had seen it and must bear a solemn witness to that truthfulness.

(Rising slowly, goes toward window, pauses there, as the lamp finally flickers out. Moonlight streams in the window)

But why should I be more select than those who have preceded me: Isaiah, and Moses. Moses! Orphan, Prince, Prophet. He gave you Aaron, Moses, even as He has given me Hyrum, trusted, faithful, wise. Still, it was you who was lifted in a cloud. You, who saw the finger writing on the stone. I think of you Moses, out of my own loneliness -- an old man, who saw the promised land and never entered it. Will it be so with me? Will I not lead my people on? Must I seal my testimony of this thing with tears, even with my blood? Would that I could deny it all, most sinful creature that I am, could go this moment to my wife, and find in her arms my reassurance, and my hope. Oh, heaven, unaware of things this truth has written on my soul, as though by lightning etched forever. Should she go, should she leave me too, as many others have, her conscience and self-pity guiding her, I must be true, with God's help, must run this course until the end.

DRAMATIC SCENE: 1M 1W • Joseph & Emma Act Two Scene 2
ABOUT THE CHARACTERS:
JOSEPH: The Prophet of the Restoration is worried about the

time he has left, about his family, friends; about this Church that God has asked him to found.

EMMA: *Is the always questioning yet wonderful support to her husband who has a job and a responsibility that no one in the modern world has ever held -- A Prophet of God. She finds it difficult to be the wife of a Prophet.*

The Mansion House. After the party. EMMA & JOSEPH, still dressed in their best clothes, are standing together. He is before a mirror, loosening his cravat. EMMA is touching a nice chair gently, thoughtfully.

EMMA: Oh, Joseph, how happy I am to have my own home at last.

JOSEPH: It does seem that we have found a place. Our enemies grow quiet.
(Pause)
The party was a great success.

EMMA: Thank you, Joseph. A woman likes these things--a home, friends, music, her own things about her.

JOSEPH: You were bred to them, my dear. I am sorry they have been so long in coming.
(He turns and studies her for a moment, then speaks softly)
But, we must not become too enamored of these things. Money, power, possessions, these are the things that in the end destroy.

EMMA: Not if they are used wisely. You have said as much yourself. I myself love this place almost with a passion. This lovely city -- the Mississippi River on three sides of us, the land rich and fruitful. But, it was not always so. By your great industry and hard work you transformed a swampland into a garden of Eden. Indeed. An island of sanctuary in an ocean of hatred and persecution.

JOSEPH: This beautiful home that has been termed "The Mansion House" -- Emma, already our own people murmur with envy ...
(JOSEPH lets EMMA untie his tie)
I am still a man.

EMMA: And such a dear man. Because I love you so there is something I must tell you ...

JOSEPH: Not bad news, I hope. Not tonight.

EMMA: It would be difficult tomorrow. And I so seldom see you alone lately. You are constantly busy.

JOSEPH: Something about the family? One of the twins?

EMMA: *(She moves away from him, sits down, fingering her handkerchief)* No, it's about you. I heard today that hatred and hostility was rising against you in the cities. They feel you are overstepping your rights... imposing your own importance... in taking part in politics. People are frightened by the militia.

JOSEPH: Do you think I'm wrong?

EMMA: No, but it would seem that religious problems would be enough.

JOSEPH: Would you compromise with the evil on all sides of us, submit as we have submitted, without any defense?

EMMA: No, but there must be some middle ground.

JOSEPH: We cannot submit. As long as a man can be locked in a prison called "Liberty Jail" while he's as innocent as a lamb, I'll fight for freedom.

EMMA: But, surely we have been persecuted enough. I thought here ... where we have been given our charter, we could live in peace, have a home.

JOSEPH: *(Going toward her, speaking seriously)* Emma, Emma, you are not beginning to doubt me, too, are you? You are not beginning to crave the comforts of security rather than the ways of the Lord? You knew it would not be easy. When your father turned against me you remained true. When others failed, you were steadfast. But even the elect, even those who have been the closest to me, have failed me. I would have staked my life on Oliver Cowdery and Sidney Rigdon. And how I longed to save them.

EMMA: What will happen to them now?

JOSEPH: I don't know as to this life. I only know that all the gifts and powers which would have been Oliver's in the life to come have been lost to him. I have conferred them to my brother Hyrum who has been loyal from the beginning.

EMMA: Why, then, wasn't he chosen to be one of the first Three Witnesses?

JOSEPH: It was not my will. And even if it had been, there would have been more doubt among the inquirers. They would have said, "Can we take his word? He is his brother. Naturally... "

EMMA: Will Oliver and Sidney reverse their testimony that they have seen the plates, handled them? Oliver was even with you.

JOSEPH: No, they're men of honor. They cannot refute what they have seen and touched -- and heard. But, they are human, and they can't help it if their humanness turns them against seeming errors. But, I swear to you, that neither they nor any of the eleven will go to their graves denying the truth of this work, and the book. To deny the power of God and his existence ... would mean damnation forever.

EMMA: I'm not really strong, Joseph. You are my strength and hope. I fear constantly that something will happen to you and the children.

JOSEPH: You don't fear too much for yourself or you wouldn't have sat alone in the buggy while I climbed the hill to get the plates.

EMMA: I was afraid. I'm still afraid. The thought of Alvin dying and his wife crossing the river carrying those two children haunts me. I ask myself over and over, "What would I do?"

JOSEPH: Poor Emma. Poor everybody whose life has been attached to mine. Forget our words.

EMMA: *(Rising with dignity)* I will. And will you, for my sake, and for the sake of the children, try to be a bit more discreet?

JOSEPH: Yes, perhaps there is some truth in what you say. Because we dared repeat that the Lord had revealed that Jackson County was to be ours the mobsters believed we were there to disinherit them all. Perhaps I can yet ease them. Their time is not yet.

EMMA: You make me very happy.

DRAMATIC SCENE: 2 boys • Joseph & Hyrum Act One Scene 2
ABOUT THE CHARACTERS:
JOSEPH: aged 10 years old has been through much physical

pain, injury and hardship with the operation on his leg at age 7 and now this. You might even call Joseph an early bloomer.

HYRUM: *aged 14 or 15 years old and the devoted friend and brother from early on to JOSEPH, whom he knows has some special something to do in his life. We see the martyrdom mirrored in this simple scene of two loving brothers. Hyrum just might be a late bloomer.*

> *The scene shows the two boys, JOSEPH & HYRUM. JOSEPH is swinging. HYRUM is leaning against a tree.*

JOSEPH: If I tried hard I could go over the top–into the sky.

HYRUM: Well, don't.

JOSEPH: But I could.

HYRUM: I think you could if you put your mind to it. I suppose you could do anything.

JOSEPH: *(Laughing)* Even get you down?

HYRUM: Maybe.

JOSEPH: Dare me?

HYRUM: Dare you!

JOSEPH: All right–run, run, Hyrum–run!
> *(JOSEPH jumps from the swing into the grass, gives a grimace which Hyrum, striking a stance, does not see. They run. They begin to wrestle. After several moments, JOSEPH has Hyrum's shoulders pinned.)*

JOSEPH: Give up?

HYRUM: *(Breathing heavily)* As usual, you've bested me, but you fight fair. You never hurt me. You're just stronger. Half the boys in Lebanon are afraid to fight you.

JOSEPH: Perhaps. But, I don't want them to be scared. And it really isn't that I'm stronger, Hyrum–I just know when I'm going to win.

HYRUM: You're pretty sure of everything. Do you have insp… inspir… inspiration–as mother calls it? I've tried…

JOSEPH: Some call it intuition. It comes swiftly. I don't try… unless you'd call praying "trying."

HYRUM: Why, we all do that. You ponder so, Joseph. You should have been the eldest in the family.

JOSEPH: No. You and Alvin are great. I'm just like mother, I suppose. She has the gift of knowing–of dreaming.

HYRUM: And she's mostly right.
JOSEPH: Yes.
> *(Pause)*

She's seems so tired lately
HYRUM: No wonder, nursing Sophronia through the typhus, getting settled here. How could you and Mother be so sure she was going to get well? I was scared.
JOSEPH: *(Meditatively)* Mother taught me once:
The heart has no room for both fear and faith:
Faith dispels fear as sun the morning mist.
Has He not told us to believe?
Fear dispels faith and is the demon, dark,
That would surely conquer and deceive.
We must kneel often. And believe.
HYRUM: I wonder you can be so wise at 10 years old.
JOSEPH: Ah… I just grow quiet. I think… and I listen.
HYRUM: I grow quiet and I fall asleep.
> *(Staring at JOSEPH)*

But Joseph, when you're in a crowd you can be so much fun.
JOSEPH: I like people, all people. But I like being alone, too. And perhaps my gaiety gets me away from my own seriousness. It frightens me. Can I tell you something?
HYRUM: You know you can.
JOSEPH: When Grandfather Smith said that one of his descendants would change the world of religion, I felt it might be me.
> *(JOSEPH cringes)*

HYRUM: But how?
JOSEPH: I don't know that. It's not that I want to… it's just a feeling.
> *(JOSEPH cringes once again. This time Hyrum notices.)*

HYRUM: What is it? Did I hurt you?
JOSEPH: No, I'll be all right.
HYRUM: But you look red in the face. You're sick.
JOSEPH: It will go away. I'm fine.
> *(He rises. His right hand pressing against his left shoulder.)*

I'm just tired. Promise you won't tell Mother?
HYRUM: I promise. But, if you get sick I will nurse you myself.

JOSEPH: Yes. But I'm feeling better already.
HYRUM: Your face is still red.
JOSEPH: Yours is too.
>*(He sinks to the ground again.)*

The worst thing about the typhus coming was that we had to quit school. You were just getting started at the Academy and us others at the neighborhood school. I liked it.
HYRUM: But there is not much they could teach you. How many times have you read the Bible?
JOSEPH: I haven't counted.
>*(Still pressing this shoulder, yet talking as though he is trying to divert Hyrum, and his own thoughts.)*

Ask something out of it. Go ahead and ask me.
HYRUM: Can't think of anything I haven't asked you already... well... where was St. Paul when he had his vision?
JOSEPH: On the road to Damascus. Do you think he was frightened?
HYRUM: I don't know. I know I would be. Especially if I'd preached against God.
JOSEPH: And worried that it might have been a dream. Do you think people believed him right off?
HYRUM: I never thought of that. I guess they didn't. People–most of them–never believed the Prophets.
JOSEPH: Think how wonderful it must have been though. To hear the voice of God?
>*(His voice lowers, he bends over.)*

Hyrum, I think I am going to be sick.
HYRUM: Oh, Joseph. Here, let me help you. I'm afraid it's the typhus. They've been expecting us to get it. I hope I don't so I can take care of you.
JOSEPH: My head's whirling. I'll lie down. Don't look so scared. I'll soon be getting you down again.
HYRUM: I hope so. But, I really don't like to fight you, even in fun. You're my best friend!
JOSEPH: And you are mine. Is that why you let me win?
HYRUM: I don't! I fight hard!
JOSEPH: I know, maybe I'm gifted as much as you say.
>*(Laughs)*

HYRUM: It's true sometimes I'm almost jealous of you.
JOSEPH: Almost. Hyrum, you'll stay with me, won't you? We

won't worry mother?

HYRUM: Of course. Take it easy-up now. Oh, Joseph, you're burning with fever. Let's get to the house.
> *(JOSEPH's head falls on HYRUM's shoulder, he nods but does not speak.)*

DRAMATIC SCENE: 2 M • Joseph & Hyrum Act Three Scene 1
ABOUT THE CHARACTERS:
JOSEPH: aged 38 years old has led a Church, a people, a family to the brink of perfection -- a place where some of them determined that they were not ready to go. He feels everything deeply, takes things personally -- he is the shepherd watching over his flock; the mother-bird tending her nestlings until they are ready to fly. The problem was that most of the nestlings were never ready to fly. Some of them even fell from the nest.
HYRUM: aged 43 or 44 years old and the brother to JOSEPH. He has been by his side -- as always -- the advisor, confidante and trusted friend. He is envied his position by others, even resented by some who wished his position for themselves. But he is true -- ever single -- to Joseph and to God.

> *A grassy spot nestled in a green wood. There is the sound of water. It is the 23rd of June, 1844 -- the day before their deaths. JOSEPH and HYRUM are together, dressed for traveling.*

JOSEPH: *(Stretching his arms wide)* Isn't it wonderful to feel free, Hyrum? To be here in the cool woods. To feel safe?

HYRUM: Yes, oh, yes.

JOSEPH: I feel almost like my old happy self. I want to laugh, to shout. Do you feel like wrestling?

HYRUM: *(Removing his coat)* If you do.

JOSEPH: Just a turn or two. I'm afraid my bones are creaking like Si Hearst's wagon.
> *(JOSEPH removes his coat and the two come toward each other, in a circle. They jockey for position and*

tussle for a moment or two and then JOSEPH lifts HYRUM over his shoulder, HYRUM in turn pulls his brother to the ground, but JOSEPH soon has HYRUM pinned by both shoulders)

JOSEPH: *(Out of breath)* Give up?

HYRUM: Yes.

(BOTH arise, brushing off the dust)

JOSEPH: I am hungry. Shall we wash and eat?

(Arms about each other they go toward the stream, returning in a moment to take a large sandwich from a large sack. They stretch themselves out as they eat)

HYRUM: *(Hesitantly)* But, Joseph ... what about us leaving like this? Is it the right thing to do when the people are in such hard straits?

JOSEPH: I know it's been bothering you. It has bothered me too. But, in the face of the new uprising of hatred and mob action, it seems the only way.

HYRUM: Yes, but remember the time we left Missouri and became ill with cholera? You prophesied then that we would return and our enemies would not even recognize us. It came true, you know. They even found us in our bed and did not know us. They passed us on the streets.

JOSEPH: Yes, yes ... Hyrum. But things are different now. Those in authority are set against us.

HYRUM: But to leave our people at their mercy.

JOSEPH: But that is the reason. Can't you see?

(Sits up)

The people are in danger because of me. It is not that I am running away. It is rather that if the mobs know that I am gone they will give up on the others. Later, when we get settled we can send for our families and friends. We can begin the work elsewhere.

HYRUM: *(Rising, walking)* The hatred since the incident over the printing press! Since we escaped from Liberty Jail. Had that editor only listened when I warned him that he must cease his assaults on us.

JOSEPH: But he would not. I was forced to go to him about his lies and his attacks upon us. He was possessed of the very devil. So much of our property, even lives, have been destroyed because of their viciousness. Our people felt justified in destroying the presses.

HYRUM: All because of your vision. And the Book of Mormon. If they only understood it they would not fear or hate it so much. The Bible tells of Christ informing the people that He had other sheep to visit.

JOSEPH: It is merely another witness to His life -- His divinity.

HYRUM: Of course they are quick to point out seeming discrepancies in it.

JOSEPH: It is not my book. It is not even God's book. It is an ancient people's book. Their record. I know that time will prove there were horses here; that it was not unusual to engrave histories upon golden sheets. It was more available than papyrus. Time will prove. Time will prove.

HYRUM: I know. I saw the plates. And now, while we are alone, Joseph, I want to tell you that I'm quite content that I was not one of the original three witnesses. People would have said I was influenced because you were my brother. It was better that it was the others.

JOSEPH: *(Taking HYRUM's hand. He doesn't know what to say for a moment)* But you are one of the six whose names will appear forever on the fly-leaf, bearing testimony to how it came into my possession.

HYRUM: You still wish to go farther?

JOSEPH: It is the only path. If only Orrin would come quickly with the horses, so that we can cross the river and be on our way before dark.

Charlie's Monument
A Musical by *Susan McCloud, Marvin Payne & K. Newell Dayley*
Based on the novel by Blaine M. Yorgason.

ABOUT THE PLAY: *Charles Langly is born with only one arm and a twisted foot, he grows to adulthood in a town that has no idea what to do with him, and is, quite frankly, embarrassed about him. They find a job as a local lookout (so what, there are no restless native tribes in the 1890s). They pay him to stay on a mountain top, where he lives his life in seclusion. The town did its duty but does not have to deal with him daily. Then love finds the lonely man. A family develops. Tragedy ensues.*

<u>SERIO-COMIC MONOLOGUE: 1M • CHARLIE Act One Scene 7</u>
ABOUT THE CHARACTER:
CHARLIE: *is the eternal optimist who is tried and tested daily in his major strength: that optimism. In this scene we find the beginning of love, the infatuation that leads to enchantment, that gives way to romance, that will develop into mature love.*

>*The Mountaintop (Hide and Seek) -- CHARLIE is lying on his stomach scanning the valley floor through a telescope.*

CHARLIE: Where is she? Not on the porch, not in her window, or the garden. It's a beautiful day. She's probably off on a picnic with some boy. I reckon the meanest thing George Reeves ever did was to send his daughter away to school. She's changed. I know she's changed. Back three days and even from here, I can tell the years have changed her. She was a friend,
>*(Composing)*

"My Smiling Angel!" Now she's ... a lady. Sprouted out all over. Ah, but if I had Nellie Reeves all to myself, just the

two of us, alone together, I'd take her hand, gently, and help her over the rough places. I'd tell her that her eyes were like summer stars. I'd say a dozen clever things to make her laugh. And she'd tell me she couldn't remember when she'd had such a good time. We'd sit quietly together then, and she'd slip her hand back into mine, and I'd tell her she was the loveliest vision... the loveliest vision my eyes had ever...
(He turns startled.)
Nellie!?

SERIO-COMIC SCENE: 1M 1W • CHARLIE & NELLIE Act One Scene 7 (Charlie's monologue again but also with the scene that follows)
ABOUT THE CHARACTERS:
CHARLIE: *is the eternal optimist who is tried and tested daily in his major strength: that optimism. In this scene we find the beginning of love, the infatuation that leads to enchantment, that gives way to romance, that will develop into mature love.*
NELLIE: *always interested in thinking in the terms of what we moderns call 'outside the box' NELLIE has climbed the hill out of curiosity, but finds oh so much more; nothing at all like she was led to believe she would find.*

The Mountaintop (Hide and Seek) -- CHARLIE is lying on his stomach scanning the valley floor through a telescope.

CHARLIE: Where is she? Not on the porch, not in her window, or the garden. It's a beautiful day. She's probably off on a picnic with some boy. I reckon the meanest thing George Reeves ever did was to send his daughter away to school. She's changed. I know she's changed. Back three days and even from here, I can tell the years have changed her. She was a friend,
(Composing)
"My Smiling Angel!" Now she's ... a lady. Sprouted out all over. Ah, but if I had Nellie Reeves all to myself, just the

two of us, alone together, I'd take her hand, gently, and help her over the rough places. I'd tell her that her eyes were like summer stars. I'd say a dozen clever things to make her laugh. And she'd tell me she couldn't remember when she'd had such a good time. We'd sit quietly together then, and she'd slip her hand back into mine, and I'd tell her she was the loveliest vision... the loveliest vision my eyes had ever...

NELLIE: *(Has appeared behind CHARLIE)* Mr. Langly!
  (CHARLIE spins. NELLIE starts)
I expect you'd stand in the presence of a lady!
  (He does. Frantically)
You know you're practically legendary. I'm surprised you're not ten feet tall! I've been away to school for years, and now that I'm back I thought I might like to meet a legend. I think it's such a victory for you to even be up here. Even I could hardly make it. But here you are, every day, watching over this town like some kind of Guardian Angel.
  (First light for CHARLIE, through the amazement and confusion)
And these rocks! Such a creative thing to do! Of course, what else could ... I mean ... well, if I were up here-uh, instead of you--I'd probably just waste all my time, oh, listening to waterfalls, collecting sunsets, reading ... writing ...
  (turning away)
memorize something ...
  (Diminuendo)
... anything ...
  (to herself)
the Sears and Roebuck Catalog!
  (Trying again)
But these rocks! They'e really so... so ... interesting. Such a remarkable person! Such challenges, such courage--and you grew up right here in Charity Bend! ... It's funny I don't remember you. That is, not very well. One's childhood memories tend to pale against the bright world out there.
  (As if to take her leave)
Well, Mr. Lang...

CHARLIE: I remember you. Nellie Reeves, the prettiest little girl in school.

NELLIE: *(Awkwardly)* Oh, you do? Fancy that!

CHARLIE: I remember you walking home along the lilacs.

NELLIE: *(Nervous now, backing away)* Is that right?

CHARLIE: And how you waited for me, once.

NELLIE: *(Frightened at the sudden intimacy--crosses hastily)* The view is ... breathtaking ... I never realized there was such a view up here!

CHARLIE: *(Offering telescope)* Here, try this.

(Coaxing. She gingerly accepts it. He places strap around her neck)

Don't drop it.

(Pointing)

Right about there.

NELLIE: There's my father!

CHARLIE: He's closing the bank for the afternoon.

NELLIE: He's scowling!

CHARLIE: He always scowls--keeps people respectful of him that way.

NELLIE: It's incredible. I can see every detail. Why, there's my ...

(Realization)

window.

(Giving CHARLIE the benefit of the doubt)

It's almost like having your own crystal ball!

(CHARLIE has been leaning in toward NELLIE, gazing at her. She turns her head toward his. Their eyes meet and they both panic. She hands him the telescope and turns quickly away, nearly strangling herself on the strap. He frantically extricates her and they spring apart)

My goodness, what the town would do if they knew... Uh, may I sit down?

(CHARLIE jumps to offer her a place to sit, spilling books from his shoulder satchel)

Books?

(Grabs a red book he is holding. He doesn't let go. Gentle tug-of-war)

You read?

CHARLIE: Write.

NELLIE: You read, right?

CHARLIE: Wrong, I write.
NELLIE: Write?
CHARLIE: My journal. The red one's my journal.
NELLIE: *(Lets go)* Oh.
 (Picks up another)
Shakespeare?
CHARLIE: I made it through the Sears and Roebuck Catalog a long time ago.
NELLIE: *(Chastened, recovers)* Do you know "Midsummer Night's Dream?"
CHARLIE: *(At last feeling an opportunity to shine, recites awkwardly)* "I'll follow you, I'll lead you about around, through briar;"
 (Checks for approval, gets it, continues, accelerating)
"Sometime a horse I'll be, sometime a hound, A hog, a headless bear, sometime a fire; And neigh, and bark, and quint, and roar, and burn!..."
NELLIE: *(Applauding)* My turn! This is the way Miss Higgins taught all the girls at school.
 (With broad sweeping gestures, very affected)
"Over hill, over dale, Through brush, through briar, Over park, over pale, Through flood, through fire, I do wander everywhere, Swifter..."
 (She forgets)
CHARLIE: *(Helping)* ... than the moon's sphere.
NELLIE: "... than the moon's sphere!"
CHARLIE: Like horse...
NELLIE: Hound ...
CHARLIE: Hog ...
NELLIE: Bear ...
CHARLIE: Fire...
NELLIE: At every turn!
 (They laugh, greatly relieved and honestly delighted. A bonding has taken place. NELLIE suddenly feels "maybe too much bonding" and turns to the book again)
YOU must have a favorite. Here's one you've underlined.
 (Reads theatrically)
"But I that am not shaped for sportive tricks Nor made to court an amorous looking glass; 1, that am rudely stamped

and want love's majesty To strut before a wanton ambling nymph; 1, that am curtailed of this fair proportion,
(Begins to appreciate meaning)
Cheated of feature by disembling nature, defo ..."
(Chokes on this word)
CHARLIE: Deformed "...deformed, unfinished, sent before my time Into this breathing world, scarce half made up, And that so lamely and unfashionable That dogs bark at me as I halt by them." (it sinks in) Boy, am I glad I'm not like him!
(Sees she is confused, still troubled)
Miss Reeves, do you know what I do when life gets dark, and narrow, and close?
NELLIE: What?
CHARLIE: Well, I think I'm gonna choke sometimes. Then I imagine a window somewhere high in a wall, with light coming through, and sometimes music even ...
NELLIE: *(Looking into the air at his illustration, as if remembering)* ... and sweet smells ...
CHARLIE: *(Stunned)* ... like moist earth ...
NELLIE: ... and a baby's breath.
CHARLIE: *(After a long moment, amazed)* Same window.
NELLIE: Have you found it?
CHARLIE: *(Letting go of the trance)* ... No. But that's what I like about this mountain. It feels a little like that window ... in my mind.
NELLIE: I'd like to know about these rocks. They must mean something to you.
CHARLIE: Well, they ... I guess I'm just trying to make something nice. I bring a stone up everyday-the prettiest one I can find.
NELLIE: That's nice. I should have expected it.
CHARLIE: *(Eagerly pointing out a rock in the waist-high pile)* Pretty, don't you think? See that streak of silver running through?
NELLIE: Nice! No ... beautiful. My father's throwing a homecoming party for me next week. The invitations are all out. I ... I know you didn't get one ... But I wish you could come. I'd better go. Thank you, Mr. Langly. Really ... thank you.
CHARLIE: Anytime! Got lots of time.
NELLIE: *(Retreats, returns, offering him the flower she has been carrying)* Here ... Charles.
CHARLIE: *(Grinning)* Charlie.
NELLIE: Charlie!

(She grins broadly, turns away and calls back from several paces down)
Bye Charlie!
(Exits)

DRAMATIC SCENE with SONG: 1M(boy of 10) 1W • CHARLIE & NELLIE Act One Scene 4
ABOUT THE CHARACTERS:
FAITH Langly: early 30s. The great picture of the nurturing, strong-for-her-family Pioneer Mother (without a husband), she has her doubts -- her fears -- but cannot let her son see them.
CHARLIE Langly: A trusting but sometimes confused at the world little boy of 10. He is definitely his mother's son. He has all her greatest qualities, and a few of his own. But he is hurt -- deep inside -- at the reactions of others towards him and his 'defect'.

The mountaintop, where most of the play takes place.
FAITH: *(appears on the valley floor, calling)* Charlie?
CHARLIE: Mama?
FAITH: *(Seeing CHARLIE)* Charlie why aren't you in school?
CHARLIE: What, Mama?
FAITH: All the other children will be in school. You'd better hurry. Charlie?
CHARLIE: But, Mama, I don't wanna go to school.
FAITH: But Charlie, you love school.
(Pause.)
CHARLIE: Mama, did those kids hurt me and make fun of me because I don't have two arms?
FAITH: *(Thoughtfully, not evasive)* Charlie, what's that picture you're drawing there in the dust?
CHARLIE: It's a deer.
FAITH: Is that all?
CHARLIE: Well, theres an Indian over there behind that rock. This line's an arrow he just shot. It's gonna hit that deer, and then the Indian'll have food for his family. He's the Papa, you know.

FAITH: I see. That's a very good picture, Charles. I wish your Papa could see it. Did you do that other one?

CHARLIE: Sure! There's the Indian dragging the deer to camp. See over there? That's his little boy running out to meet him. He sure is proud of his Papa right now!

FAITH: I'm sure his Papa is proud of him, too. Charlie, I... I can't tell you for sure why you have only one arm while all the other children have two. But I'd say God gave you only one arm because that's all He felt you needed.

CHARLIE: What do you mean, Mama?

FAITH: Why, just look at these two fine pictures you drew with your one hand. I suppose there aren't many people with two hands who could do as well. Charlie, God never makes mistakes. He made you different, but He made you special. And He expects something special from you.

CHARLIE: Well, He knows what He's doing, doesn't He?

MUSICAL # 4 -- IN A WORLD OF OUR OWN

FAITH: Yes, Charlie, He does. You can do anything in this world that really matters. And as long as we remember that, we don't have to worry about the rest of the world.
    I GUESS THE WORLD IS THROUGH WITH US,
    FORGETTING ALL THEY KNEW OF US.
    BUT WE DON'T CARE,
    AND WE WON'T SCARE,
    AS LONG AS THERE ARE TWO OF US.
    HAPPY TOGETHER,
    WE'LL MAKE OUR OWN WEATHER.
    WE'LL SING UP A SUNRISE
    AND CRY DOWN SOME RAIN.
    AND IF WE GET BOTHERED,
    OR OVERLY WATERED,
    WE'LL LAUGH UP RAINBOW
    AROUND US AGAIN.
        (Teaching)
    IN A WORLD OF OUR OWN,

CHARLIE: *(repeating)*
    IN A WORLD OF OUR OWN,

FAITH:
    WE CAN LET GO AND FLY.

CHARLIE: *(repeating)*

WE CAN LET GO AND FLY.

BOTH:
IF IT'S FUNNY, WE LAUGH.
IF IT'S LOVELY, WE CRY.
IF WE REACH FOR A STAR,
THERE YOU ARE,
HERE AM I
IN A CLOSE, QUIET WORLD OF OUR OWN.
(CHARLIE rises and gallantly invites his mother to dance.)
IN A WORLD OF OUR OWN,
WE CAN LET GO AND FLY.
IF IT'S FUNNY, WE LAUGH.
IF IT'S LOVELY, WE CRY.
IF WE REACH FOR A STAR,
THERE YOU ARE, HERE AM I
IN A CLOSE, QUIET WORLD OF OUR OWN.

CHARLIE:
IN A CLOSE, QUIET WORLD OF OUR OWN.

FAITH: Oh, I love you, Charlie.

CHARLIE: I love you, too, Mama.

FAITH: Do you feel like you can go to school, now?

CHARLIE: I'd rather stay home and play with you. They don't teach songs like that at school, Mama.

FAITH: They have lots of songs for you to learn at school. You teach me one tonight. Runners at your mark! Ready! Steady! Go!

CHARLIE: 'Bye, Mama!
(CHARLIE runs off.)

NOTE: If you choose NOT to do the song, just edit the lyrics but please finish the scene by joining the two portions of dialogue together.

Sheet music available from the Publisher in a PDF document for $1.00.

*DRAMATIC SCENE: 1F(girl of 4-9) 1M • ANNA & CHARLIE
Act Two Scene 1 (I included this short scene because even in it's lack of length it speaks volumes about parenthood, and childhood, and the human condition as it ought to be.)*
ABOUT THE CHARACTERS:
ANNA Langly: The bright and precious child who is infused with the attitudes and personalities of her parents. She is young. She is innocent. The 'world' has not happened to her -- yet. She is unspoiled and natural.
CHARLIE Langly: just can't quite believe that this precious gem of a human being was given to him. Why? But he goes about his duty to father her, because she is the 2nd love of his life.

> *Miracle -- The Mountaintop. CHARLIE and his four year-old daughter, ANNA, are flying a kite.*

ANNA: Catch the butterfly, Daddy. There it goes!

CHARLIE: Me--move fast as a butterfly? You're my butterfly, Anna. Fly to Daddy! .

ANNA: You're a daffodil, Daddy. You must hold very still or you'll frighten the little butterfly away.

CHARLIE: What if the daffodil bends in the breeze and kisses the butterfly?

ANNA: Oh, Daddy ... butterflies don't like to be kissed.

CHARLIE: But Daddies; do!
  (They kiss)

ANNA: Daddy, you be a butterfly; now.

CHARLIE: I can't be a butterfly. I have only one wing.

ANNA: *(Pointing to the sky)* Daddy, are there butterflies way up there?

CHARLIE: Better than butterflies! Hold this string and you're playing tug-of-war with angels!
  (ANNA reaches for the string)
  Well, all right. I suppose you can try it alone.
  (CHARLIE hands ANNA the string. ANNA is pulled to the brink. ANNA, unappreciative of the danger, watches the kite spiral downward. CHARLIE holds her close for a moment. She disengages and flaps off down the backside of the mountain)

ANNA: Look at the butterfly, Daddy!
  (CHARLIE watches her.)

DRAMATIC SCENE: 1F(girl of 4-9) 1M • ANNA & REEVES
  Act Two Scene 1
ABOUT THE CHARACTERS:
ANNA Langly: The bright and precious child who is infused with the attitudes and personalities of her parents. She is young. She is innocent. The 'world' has not happened to her -- yet. She is unspoiled and natural. Unfortunately, her grandfather, REEVES, is the world. ANNA has been sick.
George REEVES: Anna's grandfather, her mother's father. Bitter and surprised at the success of the little family that is growing and blooming on the mountain, despite his best efforts to get ANNA's mother to leave. Some times he can't help himself.

   Grampa -- REEVES and ANNA are walking.
ANNA: I like being outside again!
REEVES: Well, you need some fresh air.
ANNA: Grampa, why couldn't Mommy take me out?
REEVES: She's tired, honey. You kept her up most of the night.
ANNA: I didn't mean to. But every time I closed my eyes, the singing in my head started up again. And I felt so hot.
REEVES: *(Stops)* But you feel better now?
ANNA: Oh, much better, Grampa.
   (They resume walking)
  The pretty lady in my dreams said everything would be all right.
   (REEVES is puzzled)
  Grampa, look at the lilacs and the daffodils.
REEVES: You know their names? Your mother teaches you well.
ANNA: No, Daddy teaches me all the flowers' names. But Mommy says he makes some of them up. Then she laughs.
REEVES: I love your Mommy, Anna.
ANNA: Why don't you come and play with us on the mountain, Grampa? You could play butterfly with us--you and me and Mommy and Daddy. But Daddy has to play daffodil, because he only has one wing.
REEVES: Can you show me how to play butterfly?
ANNA: Oh, yes.
   (She flaps away and stumbles. REEVES rushes to her

and picks her up, gently)
REEVES: I'm sorry, Anna. I should have been more careful.
ANNA: Daddy was right. You're the best Grampa I could ever have.
REEVES: Charlie said that?
ANNA: No, Grampa, Daddy!
REEVES: *(Thoughtfully)* Perhaps I should come.
ANNA: Oh, would you?
REEVES: When would you like me to, Anna?
ANNA: Daddy says you'll come when it gets cold.
REEVES: Cold?
ANNA: When Hell freezes over.
REEVES: I ... I don't think your Daddy likes me, Anna.
ANNA: Oh, he likes everybody Grampa. Even you.
(They exit)

The Dance
A Musical by *Carol Lynn Pearson*
& *J.A.C. Redford*

ABOUT THE PLAY: Three couples meet at The Dance: Couple #1 -- Neil and Karen "the perfect married couple" to everyone but themselves; Couple #2 -- Howard, still searching for "the right one" 14 years after his mission, and Alison, a recently divorced mother of three; 'Couple' #3 -- Brad, 18, and suffering from his first broken heart, and Janet and unclaimed jewel of 23. "You come to the dance 'cause there's a chance that something good might, just might, happen tonight." is a lyric from the opening song.

<u>SERIO-COMIC MONOLOGUE: 1W • ALISON</u>
ABOUT THE CHARACTER:
ALISON: *ALISON is talking to HOWARD, an man she is interested in, but she is not yet ready for another marriage. He has never been married. Here she has been persuaded to talk about her marriage.*

NOTE: *with each new paragraph below it indicates a line of dialog cut from another character in order to form the monolog.*

ALISON: I was nineteen, went right from my father's house to my husband's house. Two years of college, but I lived at home. The only real goal I had growing up was a temple marriage, that's as far as I ever planned. Dennis came along and everything went like clockwork.
(Falters.)
I loved him. I really did -- love him. When we got married we moved into this tiny basement apartment, so little that sometimes I'd get grease spatters on his term papers, the table was that close to the stove. He laughed about it -- at first -- said it was something to remember me by in his advanced business administration classes. Am I boring

you?

He was getting a Master's. I worked as a secretary, until the first baby came. We found a little bigger apartment, still in a basement, very depressing places basements are. I tried to fix it up with the things we made in Relief Society, but it was still depressing. There was no money to do anything with. No place for Dennis to study. And then the next baby came. "Can't you keep those kids quiet? -- I've got all this studying to do." Of course I couldn't keep them quiet. So he'd leave and go to the library. One night I blew up. "I wish I had a place to run to," I said. I wish I could go to the library. You think I like being here alone with two children all day from morning until night except for three hours on Sunday and they can't even go in the nursery because they're not toilet trained yet? You think that's my idea of a good time? I wish I could go to the library!"

Nothing. He just -- went to the library. I shouldn't have said that. He wasn't having an easy time either. We had this great Relief Society lesson on seeing from the other person's point of view, walking in their moccasins. That helped me for a while. I wish he'd had the lesson too. Well. There were no more jokes about grease spatters on his term papers. There were no more jokes about anything. It's amazing how quickly you can lose your sense of humor in a basement. He stopped waking me up for a kiss when he came home late. I stopped making sure the table cloth at dinner didn't have crumbs from lunch on it. You know. Maybe you don't know.

The sad part is that at the time I did not know what I could possible do differently. But looking back I can see that wasn't true. For instance, our Relief Society President was really a sharp lady. She arranged a baby-sitting pool one afternoon a week so that anybody who wanted to could go out and do anything they chose. Can you believe that I turned it down? Everybody I knew did. It would have been admitting defeat. "If I can't take care of my own children, I'm not going to ask someone else to do it for me." Can you believe how stupid I was? Imagine the look on Dennis' face if ever he d come home and I said, "Guess what I did today? I climbed up to the Y on the mountain all by myself. Here rock I found for you, great paperweight." But no, he'd come home and see me sighing and suffering. Is it getting boring yet?

It was to Dennis. Was to me too. Home was boring. Being together was boring. All he talked about was business trends. All I talked about was diapers and the children's teeth.

Even when he couldn't use the library as an excuse anymore, there was always something else. Church -- soon he was in the bishopric. Community work -- every good cause in town needed him. When he wasn't out doing Church work, he was out saving mountains and saving the river. Before long the bishop saw what was happening. He was a great man, talked to both of us, set up a counseling program. By then it was too late. While out saving the mountains and the river -- Dennis had -- met --

(Breaks off.)

She had a family too. When I found out -- I went to stay with a friend for the weekend. I came back, and as soon as I opened the door, I knew. The record stand was empty. His guitar was gone. Everything of his was -- gone.

You know what tomorrow is?

My birthday. Today I got a card from Dennis. "Best wishes." He means it.

He was -- my whole world.

SERIO-COMIC MONOLOGUE: 1M • BRAD
ABOUT THE CHARACTER:
BRAD: is 18 and a novice, even though what he has been through was more than a first love situation. He fell hard and she didn't return his love. So, he fell harder. As with most youth, he thinks he is the only one to ever have experienced what he has gone through; or at least he is the first one in the world to feel this way.

NOTE: with each new paragraph below it indicates a line of dialog cut from another character in order to form the monolog.

BRAD: It couldn't have happened to you like this. It's never happened to anybody like this.

I heard the guys talking about some new girl that had moved into the ward, but I didn't pay any attention. Then at road show rehearsal -- I was walking toward the drinking fountain, and she was too, from the other way. We looked at each other. And suddenly it was like one of those shampoo commercials that go into slow motion with people running through the fields. After about a hundred years we both got to the fountain at the same time, looking right in each other's eyes. Wow, those eyes. Blue, like -- like the summer sky. Those eyes.

All these dumb things came into my mind to say. Like, "What are you doing for the next thousand years?" Or "Didn't we meet in the pre-existence?" But I just turned the handle of the fountain, real cool-like, and said, "Can I buy you a drink?" After rehearsal she was waiting for me outside. I knew she would be. I walked her home, and it was all slow motion again.

I was in love. I couldn't sleep. I couldn't study. All I could think about was her. And those eyes.

By that weekend, we'd planned our whole lifetime together. The kind of house we wanted. The names of our first six children. I told her I couldn't marry her until I could support her -- there would be a mission, and college. She said, "What's six years? I could wait forever for you. You're the one for me, Brad. I knew that for sure when I found those three roses in that vase on my window sill. A little voice inside me said, this is the one that I will love forever."

But I didn't give her any roses. When I told her, she looked like I'd stabbed her in the stomach and said, "I'm afraid I've made a terrible mistake."

But he gave her roses! That's why she's with him tonight, and not with me. Look at them. They're probably thinking up names for their first six children. They'd just better not use Lisa -- or Eric -- or Kevin.

(Furious.)

I sold my walkman to buy her a promise ring!

It'll never happen again. I trusted once. I loved once. And she threw me away like an old apple core. Never again.

COMIC MONOLOGUE: 1M • HOWARD
ABOUT THE CHARACTER:
HOWARD: This is a first date -- at a dance. HOWARD, in his 30s, has never been married -- has run from it, in fact -- but he loves to be around women -- sometimes. ALISON (the woman who doesn't get to speak in this monolog, but is probably also in her 30s) has just ended a disastrous, for her, marriage, when her husband left her for another woman.

NOTE: This monolog was created by cutting the one word responses from the second character. Whenever a paragraph begins anew it is where the line was cut.

HOWARD: Okay, I'll tell you the truth. I do want to get married. I know it's what I ought to do. And I want to. I've been working on it ever since I got back from my mission. Don't tell anybody, but my six months have been up twenty-eight times. That's fourteen years. I get tired of my mother introducing me as her son who never married. I get tired of her sending me newspaper clippings every time a jewelry store has a sale on diamonds. Two years ago I got so desperate that I -- . Okay. I heard somewhere how one of the brethren met his wife. He decided it was time for him to get married. He fasted three days, prayed a lot, went to this certain place, and said to the Lord, "Now the rest is up to you. The first girl I see is the one you want me to marry." In a couple of minutes a girl came walking by, he started a conversation with her, and three weeks later they were married in the temple. Great story, huh?

So I decided if it worked for him it would work for me. I fasted for three days, chose a good place. At first I was going to sit on the steps of the campus library at six a.m., but then I thought, what if she's working downtown or going to beauty school or something. I wanted to give everybody an equal chance. So at twelve noon on the big day, I got on the bus downtown, and I said "Okay, Lord, you've had three days to arrange this. I'm going to close my eyes, and at the next bus stop, the first woman to get on is the one you want me to marry."

So I closed my eyes. The bus stopped. I heard the doors open and then close. I opened my eyes. And there was a seventy year-old woman with a sack of groceries in her arms. She walked back and sat down right beside me, smiled and said, "Hello."

I took a deep breath, looked her in the eyes and said, "Lady, I'm awfully hungry. Could you spare a slice of bread?"

SERIO-COMIC SCENE: 1M 1W • BRAD & JANET
ABOUT THE CHARACTERS:
BRAD: is 18 and a novice, even though what he has been through was more than a first love situation. He fell hard and she didn't return his love. So, he fell harder. As with most youth, he thinks he is the only one to ever have experienced what he has gone through; or at least he is the first one in the world to feel this way.
JANET: is the not that much older than BRAD (at 23) but more experienced woman who has recently lost the love of her life to another woman.

BRAD: How can you hate somebody so much after you've loved them so much?
JANET: If you hate her so much now -- was it really love?
BRAD: *(Melodramatic.)* Yes, it was love! And now it's hate! Every time I look at her, I want to punch her lights out.
JANET: Both of them.
BRAD: That was so funny I forgot to laugh.
JANET: Boy, it's a good thing you didn't get married. How would you explain all that violence to your six children?
BRAD: Just be quiet and let me die.

JANET: Dying of a broken heart doesn't work, Brad. I've tried it.

BRAD: It isn't fair. The whole earth ought to open up and swallow me. That would make me happy. Very, very, very happy. Don't you hate Jay?

JANET: Of course not.

BRAD: But you might end up an old maid. You're--
(Looks around, whispers.)
twenty three years-old.

JANET: You're right. I'm getting to be what they call an unclaimed jewel.

BRAD: Aren't you worried?

JANET: That nobody will ever claim me? No. I want to get married, have children. But I'm not going to sit around and wait for some guy to come along and validate my parking ticket. If I should never get married, which I do not think will happen, there are lots and lots of wonderfully interesting things to do.

BRAD: Did you really love Jay?

JANET: Yes. I loved him. You want to hear about it?

BRAD: Sure. Misery loves company.

JANET: Well. We were really good friends for about a year. You know that.

BRAD: Yeah. You used to come over all the time to do homework.

JANET: We had a Book of Mormon class together. Well -- right in the middle of Mosiah, I fell in love with him. Only he didn't feel any differently at all. I was still just his good buddy, and I'd introduce him to my girlfriends, and tell me all about his romances. He didn't know how crazy I was about him. Finally he asked me to go to this dance and I was so excited I thought I would die. We were dancing away and he whispered, "Janet, do you believe in being a help-meet?" "Sure," I said. "Sure I do." "Great," he said, "How about helping me meet that girl over there in the green dress?"

BRAD: What a bummer.

JANET: No. He was always honest with me. Later, when his feelings did change, he was honest about that too. He grew to love me. And he let me know.

BRAD: Janet, he didn't love you. He married somebody else.

JANET: Brad, he did love me. And he married somebody else.
BRAD: That's crazy.
JANET: And true.
BRAD: Weren't you bitter?
JANET: For a while I was. Maybe a better word is -- devastated. I was going to throw myself into the Great Salt Lake, but I was afraid I might not stay under. Then I was going to join a nunnery, but the bishop wouldn't write a letter for me. So I decided just to go right on living. And it worked. See? She breathes, she moves, she dances.
BRAD: If he had loved you, it would have lasted.
JANET: You are so young. There are many shades and grades of love. And they're all nice. We learned a lot from each other. We gave a lot to each other. I know he's happy. And I know I m a better person because of him. We have only good memories of each other. I wouldn't erase it if I could.

SERIO-COMIC SCENE: 1M 1W • HOWARD & ALISON
ABOUT THE CHARACTERS:
This is a first date -- at a dance.
HOWARD, in his 30s, has never been married -- has run from it, in fact -- but he loves to be around women -- sometimes.
ALISON, also in her 30s, has just ended a disastrous, for her, marriage, when her husband left her for another woman.

HOWARD: You're a really good dancer, you know that? For a person who's as out of practice as you say you are, you're really very good.
ALISON: Thanks. I dance with my babies. I always have. I put on some good music and pick them up and away we go. They love it.
HOWARD: Lucky kids.
ALISON: But dancing with a man is -- different.
HOWARD: We're -- bigger, huh?
ALISON: Yes. And -- uh -- different.
HOWARD: You have three? Children.
ALISON: Yes. A boy and two girls. You like children?

HOWARD: *(Guarded.)* Sure. I even -- used to be one. At least, that's what my mother tells me. Hey, Alison. Look. Because this is your first date since -- since you've been dating -- I think I'd be doing you a favor to tell you something. You don't say to a guy, "Do you like children?"
ALISON: Oh.
(Sincerely.)
I'm sorry.
HOWARD: Most men would take it as a very -- leading question.
ALISON: I can see that. Thanks.
HOWARD: You want to keep things light. Tell a funny story. Got any funny stories?
ALISON: Uh. Here's one. Yesterday my little Bobby -- Oh. It's about my child.
HOWARD: That's okay. Just keep it light.
ALISON: Well, Bobby came back from washing his hands in ten seconds flat and I said, "Bobby, don't tell me you washed your hands." And he said, "I don't use soap, Mommy. I just drown the germs and wipe them off."
HOWARD: That's good. That's very funny.
ALISON: Bobby's clever. You would like him. Oh.
(She is quiet for a moment)
HOWARD: You're pretty quiet, Alison.
ALISON: Oh. I'm just trying to think of some more funny stories.
HOWARD: Relax. Just relax.
ALISON: I'll try. It's a very strange thing, you know, to be out on a date. Just having to make conversation with a man over seven -- makes me very nervous.
HOWARD: You're cute. Just say whatever happens to come to your mind.
ALISON: Howard! People never do that. I should go up to somebody and say, "Hi. I'm Alison, and I just got a divorce, and I still cry at least once a day, and I don't even like to go to Church anymore because all of a sudden I'm not a person, I'm a problem." That's what I should say?
HOWARD: You're right. Think of another funny story. Tell

you what, Alison. You've got to have your answers all ready, a whole list of them. Somebody asks what happened to your marriage, and you say, oh -- "It's better to have loved and lost. Much better."

ALISON: Really?

HOWARD: Sure. You can't just come out and suffer in front of people. It makes them -- terribly -- uncomfortable.

ALISON: I know.

HOWARD: Take me, for example. Sure, I'd like to be married, have a nice little wife and family. But I can't make a big tragic deal out of it. Ask me why I'm not married. Go ahead. I get it at least three times a week. Ask me.

ALISON: Howard, why aren't you married?

HOWARD: My intended mate was killed in the war in heaven.

ALISON: That's old, Howard. Old.

HOWARD: Ask me again.

ALISON: Howard, why aren't you married?

HOWARD: It's not my fault I'm single. I was born this way.

ALISON: *(Laughs.)* Oh, Howard.

HOWARD: Tell me I'm going to end up a ministering angel.

ALISON: You're going to end up a ministering angel, Howard.

HOWARD: Service above self! That's a good one, huh?

(ALISON laughs.)

Family
A Play by Eric Samuelsen

ABOUT THE PLAY: In Family, *real life becomes a bad weekend for the well-educated, intellectual, gospel-grounded, well-to-do Hull family. One daughter has left her husband (whom she may or may not really have shot), a son has left his mission early, and another daughter, an R.M., has left graduate school. Not exactly ideal. And their dark space monologues reveal the reality they're in is a place that they don't want to tell anyone of and almost can't speak about. Even the parents who burn the roast or buy the wrong salad have to re-decide who they are and what they mean to each other as individuals and within the family unit; that in order to move toward being Gods, which is the whole point, they each have to constantly reinvent themselves, be reborn, re-think, re-decide.*

<u>DRAMATIC MONOLOGUE: 1W</u> • *Deanna -- Act Two (the lines that have a strike through are only there for the intent and continuity and should not be spoken.*
ABOUT THE CHARACTER:
DEANNA: The daughter, caught in the middle of all the men in her life. She is a Returned Missionary who has left graduate school. Her life is not as she had planned it.

DEANNA: *(Exploding.)* I mean, I don't believe in *anything*! I mean, Seth believes in so many things. He believes, with all his heart and soul. In, you know, politics, and feminism and the environment, and gay rights. And he was in law school, actually, and he switched to social work administration, and he believes in Derrida and in Foucault and power structures in a culture and post-structuralism. And he's against war, and he's so passionate about all of it, all of it. He believes, and and and he acts on what he believes, like he marches and and and here I am, a Mormon girl from San Jose; he can hardly believe it, he's having these arguments with a Mormon, we're everything he loathes, homophobic and conservative and pro-life and anti-environment and sexist and Republican. The Christian Right. The only way he'd talk to me at all was when I told him on my mission evangelicals hated us as much as they hate what he stands for.

~~MOM: Sounds like a good liberal.~~

~~DEANNA: Yes!~~ And he's kind and he cares about people and not just abstractly, he works in a soup kitchen Saturday mornings and he, he... He wanted to sleep with me, he told me so, and when I told him I couldn't, wouldn't, he understood completely. Completely. That was Thursday, and Friday I packed and came home.

DRAMATIC MONLOGUE: 1M • Jack -- Act One
ABOUT THE CHARACTER:
JACK: he, like his family, is just regular, just trying to get by in life with as much spirituality intact as life will allow him. He has many more questions than answers, but the answers he does have he clings to in their solidity.

JACK: Nearly every evening, growing up, we'd be at the dinner table, and we'd have family history lessons, he called 'em. And he'd read everything, it felt like, and remembered everything, and it was as though, I don't know, Hammurabi or Zoroaster or Cyrus the Great were his best buddies. I mean, you seriously didn't want Dad helping you with your history homework. He'd take a black magic marker and cross things out of your textbook. They got it wrong, he'd say. And here's my Dad, and his degree's in accounting, and he's a supervisor for H and R Block. He's a tax law guy. I mean, he was on a first name basis with Hugh Nibley and Eugene England, guys at that level, and now he helps people do their tax returns for a living. But he got married right off his mission, and Mom got pregnant with Ashley his junior year at BYU, and he switched from history to accounting. Gave it up. Basically for us. And never once complained. And you've always got, you know like default mode; you can always talk to him about hockey and basically any time period in history. Yeah, I got real lucky when it comes to Dads.

DRAMATIC SCENE: 2W • Deanna & Mom -- Act Two (*The scene is on the long side. You may choose only to do part of the scene, that is your prerogative. But as a scene study in a class, it is quite full of all that is necessary for a good scene.*)

ABOUT THE CHARACTERS:

DEANNA: *makes correct choices, returns from a mission, deals with life the best she knows how and then finds that her life is not where she had panned it all those years ago. Examination is painful and she is not sure that she wants to do the examining.*

MOM: *has held her family together through the storms that come to all families. She has not wavered in public; but that doesn't mean that her private moments have been rock-solid.*

DEANNA: No, I'm fine.
>*(Awkward pause.)*

This was a really tough day, wasn't it?

MOM: Oh yeah. You remember that time, few years ago, when your father was diagnosed with cancer.

DEANNA: I remember. You told us all we had to prepare ourselves, you had some terrible news.

MOM: And it turned out to be nothing. A mistake.

DEANNA: I remember.

MOM: Your Dad and I were saying yesterday, this, having all of you come home like this, this was as bad.

DEANNA: Seriously?

MOM: Oh, yeah.

DEANNA: But we're all okay. I mean, basically, we're okay.

MOM: I suppose.

DEANNA: In fact, that's part of what I keep telling myself, that what I'm going through is not actually that big a deal. I mean, it's not like a divorce, or even Jack and his mission thing. I'm sort of, maybe, inflating it all in my head or something. I keep telling myself that, at least.

MOM: It must have been somewhat serious. Enough to come home. When you couldn't even come home for Christmas.

DEANNA: I thought about this the whole break. That's all I did, work and think about this.

MOM: We missed you.

DEANNA: I missed you too.
(Deep breath.)
Basically, it's a guy.

MOM: Someone you've been seeing.

DEANNA: Sort of. We haven't actually dated; people sort of don't date at Brown. But we talk, wonderful conversations. We go on walks, that amazing frosty air in Rhode Island. We argue.

MOM: What's his name?

DEANNA: Seth. Seth Cohen.

MOM: LDS?

DEANNA: Oh no, no, the guys in Institute, there aren't many of them anyway, and it's a real... I just didn't fit in. No, Seth's Jewish. Non-practicing.

MOM: And because of this guy, this Seth, you had to come home?

DEANNA: No, it's not like that, it's... I don't believe in anything.

MOM: The gospel, you mean.

DEANNA: No, I'm not saying that, it makes sense to me, it's comforting.

MOM: What is it, then?

DEANNA: *(Exploding.)* I mean, I don't believe in *anything*! I mean, Seth believes in so many things. He believes, with all his heart and soul. In, you know, politics, and feminism and the environment, and gay rights. And he was in law school, actually, and he switched to social work administration, and he believes in Derrida and in Foucault and power structures in a culture and post-structuralism. And he's against war, and he's so passionate about all of it, all of it. He believes, and and and he acts on what he believes, like he marches and and and here I am, a Mormon girl from San Jose; he can hardly believe it, he's having these arguments with a Mormon, we're everything he loathes, homophobic and conservative and pro-life and anti-environment and sexist and Republican. The Christian Right. The only way he'd talk to me at all was when I told him on my mission evangelicals hated us as much as they hate what he stands for.

MOM: Sounds like a good liberal.

DEANNA: Yes! And he's kind and he cares about people and not just abstractly, he works in a soup kitchen Saturday mornings and he, he… He wanted to sleep with me, he told me so, and when I told him I couldn't, wouldn't, he understood completely. Completely. That was Thursday, and Friday I packed and came home.

MOM: Well, good for you. Holding to your standards.

DEANNA: It had nothing to do with standards. I wasn't sure, I wasn't ready. It took me by surprise. Next time he asks the answer might be different. I don't know.

MOM: But you came home. Got out of the situation.

DEANNA: Mom, this isn't about chastity.

MOM: It certainly sounds to me as though–

DEANNA: Mom, tell me something. How did you get up this morning?

MOM: I don't know, Church is at nine, around seven I–

DEANNA: No, I mean how. How did you get up?

MOM: I don't understand what you're–

DEANNA: Grudgingly? Angrily? Hit the snooze alarm four or five times?

MOM: Certainly not. That's your father's way, of course. But I had to get ready. It was Sunday, and it was sure to be an awkward day.

DEANNA: Do you bound out of bed, like you can't wait to greet the day? Like, it's so exciting to be up?

MOM: I get up when the alarm sounds, because I have things to do.

DEANNA: Seth jumps out of bed. Like he can't wait to see what's in store that day.

MOM: You know this how?

DEANNA: He told me. See, he's non-practicing, but he said that it's a commandment, like the Jews have something like three hundred commandments, sort of sub commandments under the big Ten, and one of 'em is to get up excited, thrilled to be able to worship God that day.

MOM: I think I–

DEANNA: I have never in my life felt that way! Passionate, excited, energized! And especially not Sundays, where I can hardly bear to face it, Church, and all those droning dreary talks and songs too slow and... I don't *believe* in anything. Seth made me realize. No, I have a testimony. I believe in God. I find the gospel comforting, it makes sense. That's all.

MOM: I think I understand.

DEANNA: So I had to come home. I had to.

MOM: I thought you loved your major.

DEANNA: I love Dad. And Dad got pretty passionate, sometimes, about books and history and something new connection between things he'd discovered. That's the closest thing to it I've ever felt, watching Dad. Seth's like that all the time.

MOM: Jack's like that.

DEANNA: Yeah, and that's why he came home. It was making him sick.

MOM: I suppose.

DEANNA: I can't borrow... energy, passion, from Dad anymore. And it's not good for me.

MOM: In what way?

DEANNA: Oh, man, I was doing all this stuff about Emperor Yu and his magic tortoise, and I got to thinking, hey, what's the difference between believing in that and believing in Joseph and his golden plates. They both seem just as absurd.

MOM: I would say there's a big difference between–

DEANNA: And everyone wants the same thing preached every Sunday, basic doctrines. No... controversy, no disagreements, no passion.

MOM: They find it comforting. To–

DEANNA: I don't think so, I think they're just afraid. I think they're terrified. Jack says I only have an 'intellectual testimony,' and I'm going to hell because of it, and he's right, that's about all I have left, but wanting to hear the same five talks and the same four testimonies every week, that's an intellectual testimony too; you're going to hell too. Just not a very interesting one.

MOM: There's a good deal more to Church than–

DEANNA: No there is, you're right. But Mom, what am I

gonna do?
MOM: I wish I knew.
DEANNA: I miss him. I miss being around him, all that energy.
MOM: I certainly do understand that.
DEANNA: Mom, what am I gonna do?
(Pause.)
MOM: We're not, you know.
DEANNA: What?
MOM: What he says we are. What you're saying. We're not.
DEANNA: We sort of are.
MOM: I don't get up in the morning all excited to worship. I probably should, and it's probably a good idea, but I don't. But I do get up, immediately. With energy. Because there are things to do, and it's my job to do them.
DEANNA: I know, Mom, that's not the same–
MOM: I get up because I have to make the beds and maybe someone's had a baby and I have to make dinner for them, or one of the fifteen volunteer organizations I belong to or because I have my visiting teaching.
DEANNA: Mom, you don't–
MOM: In fact, the more I think about it, the more ticked off I'm getting.
DEANNA: Mom–
MOM: Don't tell me I don't have energy. Don't tell me I don't have passion. Don't tell me my testimony isn't spiritual enough just because I don't care to argue in Sunday School. Or that I'm going to hell for it.
DEANNA: I didn't say–
MOM: This Seth person, he's not here and he's not right.
DEANNA: He's sort of right.
MOM: He's not right at all!
DEANNA: He's right when he's talking about me.
MOM: No. Not true.
DEANNA: I think he is.
MOM: Deanna, do you want my advice?
DEANNA: I do, yeah.
MOM: I think you need to stick up for yourself. I think you need to show some backbone.
DEANNA: *(A bit offended.)* I don't think–
MOM: I think you should go back to Brown, and I think you

should go see this Seth, and I think you should have a good long fight with him. And don't give an inch, not on anything. Defend who you are and what you believe in, because it's worth fighting for.
DEANNA: I don't know that that's–
MOM: Because you've done nothing but back down. You've conceded every point. Haven't you?
DEANNA: No!
MOM: You can too get passionate about the gospel. I know you can, because I've seen you.
DEANNA: Not for a long while.
MOM: Because you're embarrassed. "Just a Mormon girl from San Jose." Nonsense. You're my daughter, and your father's daughter, and you're a returned missionary, and you're not some little Mormon mouse. You've let Brown University intimidate you. Get over it.
DEANNA: It's not easy.
MOM: You want it to be.
DEANNA: I never said that I wanted an easy road.
MOM: But you do want it to be more exciting.
DEANNA: I think there's something wrong with a culture that–
MOM: Never mind that!
DEANNA: No, but I think that there is.
MOM: Well, what have you done about it? I say, defend the faith, and you'll feel the passion.
DEANNA: I wish I knew.
MOM: And conservative, you let him call you a conservative!? Excuse me, but I have been Democratic precinct captain for San Jose Eighth for fourteen years! Nobody calls me a conservative!
DEANNA: No, that's true.
MOM: Go back to Brown. Go back to Seth. And fight with him. And make it a good fight. A hard fight. Let him know he's been in a tussle.
DEANNA: If I do, there's a pretty good chance I'll end up wanting to marry him.
MOM: We'll cross that bridge when we come to it.
DEANNA: I don't know that I can stay in that major.
MOM: Well, what other majors have you considered?
DEANNA: *(Laughing, a little.)* You're putting this all back on me, in other words.
MOM: Yes. I am putting it all back on you. Your father is

upstairs. You need to tell him what you told me, about your major.

DEANNA: I will.

MOM: Deanna. On your mission, you told me, in Taipei, you taught a first discussion to a young woman you saw sitting on a park bench.

DEANNA: I remember.

MOM: A first discussion, about Joseph and the plates. The story you say now reminds you of Emperor Yu's tortoise.

DEANNA: Yes.

MOM: And then the Spirit told you to challenge her to baptism. And you did.

DEANNA: And she accepted. Fifteen minutes after we met her. Chen Wei, I got a letter from her a couple months ago. I know where you're going with this.

MOM: Who was the girl who taught that discussion?

DEANNA: Mom, I don't know her anymore.

MOM: Well, you should reintroduce yourself. Because she was, and is, terrific.

Fire In The Bones
A Play by *Thomas F. Rogers*

ABOUT THE PLAY: The story of the Mountain meadows Massacre and John D. Lee. The play, again, is a trial. The play suggests the tragic dilemma into which well-meaning persons like John D. Lee are sometimes thrust -- and -- the sacrifices that a community, right or wrong, may require of them. FIRE IN THE BONES is a study in tainted conscience and mob psychology. In their temperament and their fate, its characters resemble the zealots of every society and age. Such people -- ancient or modern -- make tragedy as timely as ever.

<u>*DRAMATIC MONOLOGUE: 1M • Haight -- Act 1, Scene One*</u>
ABOUT THE CHARACTER:
HAIGHT is one of the unhappy conspirators who is trying to absolve himself of any responsibility.

HAIGHT: *(suddenly furious)* That will not do, Colonel Dame. You know that you issued the orders to wipe out these people, and you cannot deny it! Nothing has been done except by your orders, and it is too late in the day for you to go back on the men who carried them out. If you think you can shift the blame for this onto me, you're wrong. I did nothing except what you ordered done. And I, for one, will not be lied on. You'll stand up to your orders like a man, or I'll send you to Hell cross lots! You cannot sow pig on me!! The trouble is this, Major Lee: Colonel Dame ordered me to do this thing, and now he wants to back out and lay it all on me. He cannot do it! He shall not do it! I shall blow him to Hell before he shall lay it all on me... ! He has got to stand up to what he did like a man. He knows he ordered it done, and I dare him to deny it.

DRAMATIC SCENE: 1M 1W • John D. Lee & Emma -- Act 1
ABOUT THE CHARACTER:
JOHN: The man who has the burden of guilt, whether he is guilty or not, he ends up dying for it.
EMMA: his wife

EMMA: What's all this talk about last September, John?
JOHN D.: It's nothing, Emma. Just a little trouble the Indians gave some gentiles that were passing through.
EMMA: Oh, yes. I remember now.
JOHN D.: Remember? Remember what... ?
EMMA: Oh, nothing.
JOHN D.: You're sure?
EMMA: Quite sure, dear.
JOHN D.: It didn't affect the Saints much, thank heaven. I'll tell you about it sometime. But not right now. Today's especially set apart for just you and me.
EMMA: *(taking his arm and beaming at him)* The most important day of my life, John D. Lee!
JOHN D.: How young I feel again--young and innocent--with you by my side.
EMMA: How secure and strong I am with your arm around me.
JOHN D.: You're very special, Emma. If you were my only wife, you couldn't be more special.
EMMA: I couldn't imagine ever marrying anyone besides you, John D. That's why I'm willing to share you with the others.
JOHN D.: You're sure of that?
EMMA: Quite sure.
JOHN D.: I still can't understand why the Lord blessed me so-- what made a young beauty like you fall in love with an old man like me?
EMMA: I knew it when I first laid eyes on you--that night in Salt Lake, at the meeting. I knew you were the one for me as soon as you started to pray. I wondered how long it would take before you saw me in the audience.
JOHN D.: But you never seemed to look up. I could tell you knew I was smiling at you, but you wouldn't look up. And when it was over, you ran away.
EMMA: I guess I was a little scared. And then I figured that, if you really wanted to, you could find me.

JOHN D.: And I did, Heaven be praised.
(He kisses her.)
How I love you .
EMMA: How I love *you*...
JOHN D.: Now let's go tell the Lord and seek his benediction.
EMMA: His eternal benediction, John D.
JOHN D.: That's right, my dear, for now and ever after.
(They go offstage.)

<u>*DRAMATIC SCENE: 2M • JOHN D. Lee & George Albert SMITH -- Act 2 Scene Three*</u>
ABOUT THE CHARACTER:
JOHN: the man who bears the guilt of the Mountain Meadows Massacre, whether he deserves it or not. A staunch Saint, true to his Church and his God.
SMITH: an Apostle, a good man in a difficult position.

GEORGE ALBERT SMITH: *(joining John D. on the bench)* How are you, John?
JOHN D.: Never thought I'd see you here.
SMITH: Was passing through. Had a spare hour. Knew exactly where to find you. So here I am.
JOHN D.: Anyone send you?
SMITH: Not really. Just missed my old friend. Thought I'd try to cheer him up a little.
JOHN D.: You're a kind hearted cuss, George Albert. As kind a man as ever lived. I remember how you talked to your sick oxen, crossing the plains, offering them melted snow and feeding them handfuls of grain. Couldn't stand to kill one of them that was shot up by the Indians, or witness while we put it out of its misery. Then you took those very Indians to your tent, saw how miserable and hungry they were, offered them bread and finally gave them you dead ox in exchange for that emaciated child of theirs so you could clothe and feed him.
SMITH: You were always good to the Indians too, John.
JOHN D.: Too good, it seems.
SMITH: I didn't mean that.

JOHN D.: I know. But since those days, I have waded through trouble, George Albert--more than my share, I think--and passed through dark and trying hours. Not that you haven't too. You lost George Albert, Jr.-- how long ago now?

SMITH: Fifteen years exactly.

JOHN D.: To other Indians.

SMITH: Yes. You comforted me then...

JOHN D.: As for me, forgive me, George Albert, but many who should have been my friends have put their feet upon my neck--not you and not Brother Brigham, God bless you. Way back in Winter Quarters Brother Brigham said that no man in this church had done as much for the soldiers' wives and the poor widows as Brother Lee, and Heber C. Kimball said one time, "In the name of Israel's God, this man Lee who now is so much spoken evil of will yet destroy and trample under his feet, and walk over their graves, those that would destroy him."... And they haven't forgotten. They do remember me, don't they? Don't you, George Albert?

SMITH: Yes, we do

JOHN D.: Well, my trials have taught me at least one thing.

SMITH: What's that?

JOHN D.: Patience. Earlier I had zeal but not according to knowledge. I wanted to do good but didn't know how to bear with folks, and so I gained their ill will by my own folly. I figured others wouldn't resent me if I thought well of them. I never remember feeling malice toward another man, George Albert.

SMITH: I believe you, John.

JOHN D.: And that's why I figured--for all my shrewdness in other ways-- that others were that way too. I didn't know that there were so many warm water Saints. But I was wrong.

SMITH: You still have friends.

JOHN D.: I know.

SMITH: Like Isaac knew that his father Abraham still loved him.

JOHN D.: Yes?

SMITH: You know that Brother Brigham still loves you, don't you, John D...?

JOHN D.: What do you mean?

SMITH: It's terribly important that, now you've been imprisoned and must stand trial, you win this one.

JOHN D.: Yes. Of course. I hope I will. But either way he'll support me, won't he? Abraham didn't sacrifice Isaac after all, did he?

SMITH: Isaac wasn't sacrificed, it's true. But he was sacrificed. And had it been necessary...

JOHN D.: But he owes me that, doesn't he?

SMITH: Owes you? Owes you what, John D...? I understand how hard it must have been, dear friend, to face up to it all, but, you remember, when you first reported to us about the massacre...?

JOHN D.: Yes?

SMITH: How you perjured yourself before President Young?

JOHN D.: Perjured??

SMITH: How you told him it was the Indians who were entirely responsible. How you named no white men, not even those who came to bury the dead...?

JOHN D.: There may have been some things I didn't say then. I didn't try to make myself look any better--or any worse--than the rest.

SMITH: Still there was information you didn't give him.

JOHN D.: Did he want it??

SMITH: Probably not. But if he'd had it, he might have known better, sooner, how to act...

JOHN D.: But what, George Albert, of all your rabble-rousing speeches about Johnston's Army and Brigham's pow-wow with the chiefs? Don't you suppose that made some difference too?

SMITH: It's possible.

JOHN D.: And that's all?

SMITH: John. It's you who are on trial. Not me. Not Brother Brigham.

JOHN D.: Not any of the rest of you as long as I stay on trial, you mean. I and no one else. As long as they pinpoint the blame on some no-count Indian farmer. That way I still serve the cause, don't I? Is that why, after I was cut off, folks still occasionally spoke of my... "mission"...?

(Smith does not reply.)

When did you first think I was... that I and the others were implicated?

SMITH: It's hard to say. We didn't like to talk--or think--about it. Dwelling on it, brooding wouldn't help the Saints to prosper or survive... John, remember Brother Brigham's advice, that helped us get across the plains and withstand all the other crises thus far--"Keep your face to the setting sun."

JOHN D.: "The night is short and will pass as a dream."

SMITH: John, everything you ever did, you did to build the Kingdom, to aid the people in their troubles. We know that. You never turned a hungry person from your door, did you?

(John D. weeps, silently. After a long interval Smith takes his hand, pats his shoulder and stands. John D., still weeping, does not respond.)

I must go, John.

(He moves away from the bench in the direction he came from. He is nearly off the stage when John D. speaks.)

JOHN D.: George Albert?
SMITH: Yes, John.
JOHN D.: Say hello to Brother Brigham!

The Forge and the Fire
A Musical By *Max C. Golightly*, and others.

ABOUT THE PLAY: a series of LDS vignettes and songs that testify to the divinity of Christ and his restored Gospel. Powerful serious and familiar comic playlets are interspersed with a hilarious pair of dutiful missionaries who keep "Knockin' On Doors"

DRAMATIC MONOLOGUE: 1W • Pioneer Woman -- Act 1
ABOUT THE CHARACTER:
PIONEER WOMAN: We know little more about her than what is in her monolog. This is her only appearance in the play. But she is talking to us about her grief at losing her two year-old daughter. She could be any age under thirty, she represents every mother.

PIONEER WOMAN: We were members of a wagon train from Ohio to Salt Lake City, camped in the desert one evening, enjoying dancing in the circle to a fiddler's music. We were shocked, then terrified when we discovered that our two-year old daughter, Jennie, had wandered from our wagon and was lost. We spent the night and most of the next day searching for her.

It was November and winter would soon be setting in. To stay on the prairie when the snows came, might mean hunger -- freezing to death, and though the members of the wagon train were as disturbed and mystified as we were, we knew they were anxious to be on their way. My husband wanted to stay behind while the others went on, to search further; finally, as the last of the searchers returned, and after much praying, he gave them leave to move on.

Looking back, I don't know how we left without Jennie. What had happened, seemed impossible -- more than we could endure! As our wagons left the campsite, we sat in our wagons, looking back for as long as we could see,

shedding copious tears. There was an ache in our breast that would never go away.
(PAUSE)
We never knew what happened to her.
I often wonder if I could bear that hurt again. Could you?

<u>DRAMATIC MONOLOGUE (with song): 1W</u> • <u>Contemporary Woman -- Act 1</u> (the song is optional)
ABOUT THE CHARACTER:
CONTEMPORARY WOMAN: *Another character who's only appearance in the play speaks of the tragedy in her life. But she is not a Pioneer in the sense that she crossed the plains. She, again, this modern woman, is a representation of every member who has ever doubted during the trials of their life.*

CONTEMPORARY WOMAN: When my handsome and vital husband was pronounced a hopeless cancer victim at 42, I questioned justice, God's wisdom -- whatever there was to question. We had two young children who needed a father. We had struggled as all young couples do, and life was beginning to look rather bright economically. Now we must accept the fact that there was no future at all for him. I watched his fight to live, growing weaker in his desperation, then his ultimate surrender. I watched him grit his teeth with pain, talked with him about nothing, feigned light-heartedness, counting the minutes until his next shot. I saw the bewilderment in the eyes of his children and in his own.

I cursed, I cried, I prayed -- and he died! So many people came...so many kind people, trying as I had done so many times, to say the right things to comfort me. One old friend took my hand and said: "How blessed you are! You have so many experiences in life the rest of us may never have."

I was shocked, then angry and finally, perplexed that he would say a thing like that at such a time. But I couldn't forget his words; they would come into my head at the strangest moments. But little by little, through other struggles equally difficult, I felt the strength that only experience can give to us, and I understood -- came to realize how true that statement was! "How blessed you are!" he had said, "You have had so many experiences in life the rest of us may never have. "I <u>was</u> blessed, tragic and unhappy experiences remain tragic when we hold on to them in that way, when we do not try to understand them and accept their place in our lives. When tragedies are given the proper perspective -- not a dominant place, it leaves room for healing and for good things to grow and flower there.

SONG -- THERE IS NO DEATH (optional)

SOLO:
> THERE IS NO DEATH
> THERE IS NO DEATH,
> THE STARS GO DOWN TO RISE UPON SOME FAIRER SPHERE.
> AND BRIGHT IN HEAVEN'S JEWELED CROWN
> THEY SHINE FOREVER,
> THEY SHINE FOREVER MORE.
> THERE IS NO DEATH,
> THE LEAVES MAY FALL,
> THE FLOWERS MAY FADE AND PASS AWAY,
> THEY ONLY WAIT
> THROUGH WINTERY HOURS
> THE COMING OF THE MAY.
> AND VERY NEAR US, THOUGH UNSEEN,
> THE DEAR IMMORTAL SPIRITS TREAD,
> FOR ALL THE BOUNDLESS UNIVERSE IS LIFE.
> THERE IS NO DEATH.

Sheet music available from the Publisher in a PDF document for $1.00.

COMIC SCENE: 1M 1W • Oliver & Martha -- Act 1
ABOUT THE CHARACTERS:
OLIVER: College-age and still full of what life has to offer. And what a pick-up line.
MARTHA: College-age, guarded and suspicious, but easily won-over by people who are genuine.

OLIVER: Can I ask you a simple question? Who're you mad at?

MARTHA: *(Wide-eyed look)* Men.

OLIVER: Ah! Well, that's good! Everyone ought to be mad sometimes -- so they know what a nice thing it is not to be mad.

MARTHA: That's very philosophical.

OLIVER: *(After a pause)* That a good book?
 (Looking at title.)
 Is it about women?

MARTHA: About men.

OLIVER: It says it's about women.
 (SHE looks at the cover, continues reading.)
 It must be about women.

MARTHA: What's wrong with women?

OLIVER: Nothing -- my mother was one.
 (OLIVER grins.)

MARTHA: *(not smiling)* Why are you bothering me?

OLIVER: I'm not bothering -- I'm talking. Would you like me to go away?

MARTHA: Probably. I want to know why you're talking to me?

OLIVER: I like you.

MARTHA: How can you like me, you just met me!

OLIVER: Yeah!
 (HE grins.)
 I haven't even met you yet, and I still like you.
 (SHE turns away, amused.)

You really have spunk, don't you?

MARTHA: Spunk? That's my nicest compliment of the day.
(SHE cant help but laugh a little.)

OLIVER: You have a nice laugh, too.

MARTHA: *(beginning to warm)* That wasn't a laugh -- it was a smirk!

OLIVER: You have a nice smirk!

MARTHA: *(Grinning like him)* You know, you really have a line and a half!

OLIVER: But -- you like it?

MARTHA: I didn't say that. It's a lot like any other line.

OLIVER: And a half -- !

MARTHA: You win! What's your name?

OLIVER: Is that by way of encouragement?

MARTHA: It's by way of conversation. You're not as bad as some guys I know.

OLIVER: That's encouragement -- of a kind. Do you have a boyfriend?

MARTHA: Are you always this frank?

OLIVER: I'm Oliver.
(SHE laughs)
That's corny. I'm sometimes corny.
(THEY laugh together)

MARTHA: Thanks for telling me.

OLIVER: Do you?

MARTHA: Do I what?

OLIVER: Have a boyfriend?

MARTHA: You're unbelievable.

OLIVER: Now you're overdoing it. What else is in the book?

MARTHA: You really want to know?

OLIVER: I'm always curious about what women have to say about men.
(Opens the book to the first chapter and reads, sexily.)
"Comparison of Male Sex Appeal Personality Factor with Women" Wow! Is it good?

MARTHA *(Completely won over)* It's getting better!
(Throws the book over her shoulder.)

Zion BookWorks

Huebener
A Play by *Thomas F. Rogers*

ABOUT THE PLAY: The inspiring and tragic story of Helmuth Huebener(17) who, along with Rudi Wobbe(16), and Karl-Heinz Schnibbe(18), and Jonni Duewer(17) stood up against the propaganda machine of the Nazi Rise to power in Germany of World War II, and the price they paid for their true patriotism and Faith in God.

<u>DRAMATIC MONOLOGUE: 1M</u> • <u>Helmuth -- Act 2 Scene Five</u>
ABOUT THE CHARACTER:
HELUMTH is a sixteen year old member of the Church of Jesus Christ of Latter-day Saints who comes to learn how much his testimony means to him as he charts his unalterable course to stand up for what he believes in.

>*This monolog ends the play. October 27, 1942. A cell at the Gestapo prison and execution site in Ploetzensee, Berlin. HELMUTH sits on a bunk, writing on a note pad.*

HELMUTH: My dearest family, when you receive this letter I will be dead. But before my execution I have been granted one wish: to write to my loved ones.... I am very thankful to my Heavenly Father that this agonizing life is coming to an end this evening. I could not stand it any longer. My Father in Heaven knows that I have done nothing wrong. I am only sorry that in my last hour I have to break the Word of Wisdom. I have only two hours left. Then I must appear before my God. The appeal, initiated by yourselves and others courageous enough to take my part, did not succeed; but I did not expect that it would.... It is possible that I might have said or done certain things that could have helped mitigate my sentence without further endangering the other defendants. But I felt much as did Luther at Worms: "Here I stand. God help me, I can do no other...." And also like the Prophet Joseph as, returning to Carthage, he declared: "I am going like a lamb to the slaughter, but I am as calm as a summer's morn. I have a conscience void of offense toward God and toward all men. If they take my life, I shall die an innocent man, and my blood shall cry from the ground for vengeance, and it shall be said of me, 'He was murdered in cold blood.'" Truly, though life is precious—just how precious one only fully understands at a moment like this—precious, and I and life about to part company, I would not change my course, had I to do it over. My only regret is the sorrow and anguish I have caused all of you. Greet all the members for me. And tell Bruder Zoellner... tell Bruder Zoellner that, even if he did denounce me, I forgive him. I plead for his forgiveness and that of any others whom I have caused anxiety or difficulty. Lastly, be assured of my love and my testimony of the gospel and the restored Church... I know that God lives and that He will be the proper judge of this matter... May our Heavenly Father bless us all to be worthy of His presence when we meet again... Until our happy reunion in that better world, I remain, Your Helmuth.

DRAMATIC SCENE: 2M • Helmuth & Rudi-- Act 1 Scene Two
ABOUT THE CHARACTERS:
HELMUTH: age 17, can see nothing but what is right, even in a world that never seems right.
RUDI: age 16, while he is dedicated to the ideals that his Faith teaches, he is conflicted by his fears but loyal to Helmuth.

RUDI: *(first looking about to be sure they cannot be overheard)* I really didn't want to talk about my Sunday School class.
HELMUTH: I could tell.
RUDI: It's...that radio we've been listening to.
HELMUTH: I'm sorry, Rudi, but I won't have time this evening—not with Gerhard here.
RUDI: I didn't mean that.
HELMUTH: But if you'd like to take it, I'll trust you. I could give you the branch house key. You'd be perfectly safe listening to it there.
RUDI: Thanks, Helmuth, but it's not that.... I...I just don't think we should listen to it anymore.
HELMUTH: I see.

RUDI: After all, it's against the law.
HELMUTH: I know.
RUDI: And it's dangerous.
HELMUTH: I know that too. Rudi, it frightens me as much as you. But...you know I've been transcribing some of those BBC broadcasts. I've written them down—here, they're in my vest pocket.
RUDI: No. Don't show them to me. Not here. And don't pass them around. It's too dangerous.
HELMUTH: I won't. I'll burn them, I guess, after I've studied them some more. But I've also compared them with our news broadcasts, and that's what really bothers me.
RUDI: What does?
HELMUTH: The detail.
RUDI: Detail?
HELMUTH: Ja. The BBC has so much more detail. It gives the exact times and locations of bombing raids.
RUDI: They could still be lies.
HELMUTH: Not what they say about Hamburg. It's exactly as we've seen it here. With no exaggeration.
RUDI: That's because they've done so much damage. Naturally they'd take credit for it.
HELMUTH: But they also give the statistics on our bombings over London, and their losses are just as heavy.
RUDI: Which means we're not doing so badly after all.
HELMUTH: It's not that. It's just that our broadcasts never admit to any defeat. In ours we're always victorious. It's all too one-sided. I wouldn't have noticed it so much except for the contrast. The British version is always more balanced, more objective, more truthful, while ours...ours...
RUDI: Not truthful?
HELMUTH: Worse...full of lies. Deliberate lies, I'm afraid.
RUDI: But, Helmuth, what can you do about it? A junior grade clerk in the State Welfare Office? What good can you do, even if you shout it from the rooftops? No one will dare listen. And before you can say two words they'll crush you.
HELMUTH: I know.
RUDI: So don't be stubborn. Don't be stupid. It won't do any good.
HELMUTH: I know....

Jedediah!
A Musical by *James G. Lambert* and *C. Michael Perry*

ABOUT THE PLAY: The story of Jedediah Morgan Grant, father of Heber J. Grant and a true pioneer. Their accomplishments, their strength of character and their perseverance in the face of uncommon trials, depredations and hardships has few equals in the history of man.

<u>SERIO-COMIC SCENE: 1M 1W</u> • *Jedediah GRANT & SUSAN Noble -- Act 2*
ABOUT THE CHARACTERS:
GRANT: *still young, is excited about life in Salt Lake City. His first wife has died and he is looking for another; someone to be more than a mother to his children, but a companion for him.*
SUSAN: *Has known Jed since she was quite young. They crossed the plains together. She has other suitors, much younger than Jedediah, but her closeness and affinity for him is a leading factor in her decision.*

SUSAN: What is it, Jedediah?
GRANT: Solomon Westbridge is here demanding an answer to his proposal. I want you to go down and tell him "no"!
SUSAN: I have no intention of doing that!
GRANT: Why not? You don't love him, do you?
SUSAN: I don't believe that you have the right to ask that question.
GRANT: I disagree.
SUSAN: And just what gives you the right to interfere?
GRANT: The right of a man who loves you.
SUSAN: You had better explain just what you mean by that!
GRANT: I said, "I love you, Susan -- and I want you to marry me.
SUSAN: Do you really mean that -- or am I just a convenience you don't want to lose?
GRANT: I guess I deserve that, Susan—because I've fought

ever telling you before. But I want you to believe me. I've never meant anything more in my whole life.

SUSAN: I've waited so long to hear you say that—it's hard to believe you finally have. Especially when you kept turning down the Councils call to Plural Marriage.

GRANT: You would have agreed to that?

SUSAN: *(Nods)* I love you, Jed. I always have.

GRANT: If the call came again, would you consider plural marriage now?

SUSAN: Why?

GRANT: Because today Brigham asked me to consider it again. He even suggested I marry both you and Rosetta.

SUSAN: And what did you tell him?

GRANT: That I'd consider it, but that I wanted to marry you regardless -- if you'd have me.

SUSAN: What about Rosetta?

GRANT: That decision is yours, Susan, not mine.

SUSAN: You do love her, don't you?

GRANT: Yes, but not with the urgency that I love you. She brings me peace and tranquility.

SUSAN: Well, what do I bring you -- war and hostility?

GRANT: No. You have an exciting combustibility. You always keep me guessing.

SUSAN: I see, Jeddy. Well, about Rosetta -- I don't know. I would have to think on it. So, if you'll take me on those terms, I'll accept your proposal.

GRANT: Just so our commitment is secure.

SUSAN: It is, Jedediah, it is!

(They embrace)

I'd better go down and dispatch Solomon one last time. Will you wait here?

GRANT: If you wish.

SUSAN: I'll be right back.

Liberty Jail
A Musical by *Orson Scott Card* and *C. Michael Perry*

ABOUT THE PLAY: At the end of the persecutions of the Mormons in Missouri, Joseph Smith, Hyrum Smith, Sidney Rigdon and three others were imprisoned in a jail at Liberty, Missouri. The conflicts that arose there and the friendships that were formed shaped the future history of the Mormon Church — and also brought to Mormon Scripture the beautiful and poetic Section 121 of the Doctrine and Covenants.

<u>DRAMATIC SCENE (with optional song)</u>: *2M • ALEX MacRae & SIDNEY Rigdon -- Act 1 (The song is optional)*
ABOUT THE CHARACTERS:
ALEX: *a youth, probably younger than current mission age who is devoted to the Prophet Joseph as much as he is to Christ.*
SIDNEY: *cast by many as not only a great religionist, but a flawed and self-interested man who got the Church into plenty of hot water. He eventually left the Church when Brigham Young took over the role that Sidney desired -- Prophet.*

SONG -- A PLACE WITHOUT SUN

ALEX:
IN A PLACE W ITHOUT WINDOWS.
IN A PLACE WITHOUT SUN.
WE FORGET ABOUT DAYLIGHT.
WE FORGET HOW TO RUN.
WE FORGET HOW TO HURRY.
WE FORGET HOW TO HATE.
WE ENDURE ALL THE WORRY.
WE LEARN HOW TO WAIT.
WHEN THERE'S NO PLACE TO GO
AND NOTHING TO SEE
TIME DOESN'T MATTER

IN CHAINS YOU ARE FREE --
AT LIBERTY -- IN JAIL
WE ENDURE ALL THE WORRY
WE LEARN HOW TO WAIT.
WHEN THERE'S NO PLACE TO GO
AND NOTHING TO SEE
TIME DOESN'T MATTER.
IN CHAINS YOU ARE FREE
AT LIBERTY-- IN JAIL

(At the end of the Song Alex has come downstairs)

SIDNEY: Alex, you look worried -- or upset.

ALEX: Brother Rigdon -- I -- no, I was just --

SIDNEY: Is your family in any danger?

ALEX: I don't know. I haven't heard.

SIDNEY: Poor fellow.

ALEX: I never knew people could be so ugly! The mobs, the cruelty of it all --

SIDNEY: Men have always been evil.

ALEX: But - I never knew how strong and good people could be either. Until that night at Richmond jail, before the trial - remember how the guards were talking? And then Joseph stood -

SIDNEY: Alex, don't worry, most of those stories were probably lies

ALEX: Oh, they're true enough. All true. But, you see, when Joseph stood up like that and spoke with the power of God, I felt like -- I felt like everything was worth it. Everything would work out in the end. Because God was still with the Prophet

SIDNEY: I wish all men could have your faith.

ALEX: Me? Oh, I'm just a nobody.

SIDNEY: You have the same eternal potential as --

ALEX: Oh, no, Brother Rigdon I'm not the sort that ever becomes famous or important. I expect I'll always just sort of make a living and go to Church. Maybe someday they'll ask me to go on a mission or something.

SIDNEY: You have a dismal view of your future.

ALEX: I'm happy with it. That's the way I want to live. I'm not the sort who's happy telling other people what to do. I don't know what they should do.

SIDNEY: Does anyone after all?

ALEX: I don't know anymore. Brother Rigdon. Lyman Wight's been telling me things.

SIDNEY: Oh, Lyman.

ALEX: Why, is he lying?

SIDNEY: Depends on what he said, doesn't it?

ALEX: He said -- he was a member of the Danites.

SIDNEY: Oh!? Did he now!

ALEX: And not only that, he said that you and Joseph knew about the Danites. How they was out robbing the-Gentiles and burning down houses. And if that's true -- why, no wonder the gentiles hate us! Those Danites brought all this down on us!

SIDNEY: Satan brought all this down on us, Alex. Don't you know? The Gentiles always hate the Saints. It's the way of the world.

ALEX: That's not what I'm asking! I want to know if Joseph Smith knew about them! And you -- Lyman said you gave a speech to them!

SIDNEY: There are times, Alex, when violence is the Lord's way. The Lord of the New Testament as well as the old. I come not to bring peace but a sword

ALEX: Then Samson Avard was telling the truth and you were lying to everybody.

SIDNEY: Alex, Avard's testimony was so full of lies that I don't think anyone will ever know where the lies leave off and the truth begins.

ALEX: Did you know about the Danites?

SIDNEY: Alex, I can honestly tell you that Joseph Smith never started any such group of men. The Mormon Church is a law-abiding Church.

ALEX: But you -- did you know about the Danites

SIDNEY: I never heard of them until Samson Avard talked about them on the stand.

Sheet Music available from the publisher for $1.00 in PDF format.

DRAMATIC SCENE (with optional songs): 2M • JOSEPH Smith & HYRUM Smith -- Act 1
ABOUT THE CHARACTERS:
JOSEPH: *The boy whom God trusted with the Restoration of His gospel, imperfect but always yearning to know the ways of truth. He is now in his 30s and feels that God has not spoken to him because of something he has done.*
HYRUM: *Joseph's confidante, his ever-faithful, long-suffering companion, his exterior conscience.*
This is a complex scene and is quite satisfying as a whole. But you can use the song into the dialog, or use the dialog into the second song, or use the entire piece, or just the dialog.

SONG -- WHEN DID THE MAN BECOME A PROPHET?

JOSEPH:
WHEN DID THE MAN BECOME A PROPHET?
WHEN DID THE BOY BECOME A MAN?
WHO CAN TAKE A HOLD OF HEAVEN?
NOBODY CAN. NOBODY CAN!

WITH THE SUN RISING IN THE TREES.
WITH A STORM OF LIGHT
YOU CAME TO THE BOY
THERE ON HIS KNEES.
FROM THEN ON, FATHER,
I'VE FOLLOWED YOUR HAND
WHEREVER YOU'VE LED ME,
WHATEVER YOU'VE PLANNED.
BUT WITHOUT THE MEN I'VE LOVED TO HOLD ME.
HOW CAN I STAND?

YOU KNOW WHO I AM.
KNOW THAT I'M NEVER WISE
UNLESS YOU OPEN MY EYES, FATHER
SHOW ME YOUR PLAN
I AM A MAN WHO NEEDS
TO KNOW HOW THE SEEDS WILL GROW'

SEGUE TO
SONG -- HE'S YOUR FRIEND (reprise)

HYRUM:
HE'S YOUR FRIEND, HE'S YOUR FATHER,
HE'S YOUR BROTHER, HE'S YOUR SON
HE'S YOUR

JOSEPH:	**HYRUM:**
PLEASE	FRIEND, HE'S YOUR FATHER, HE'S YOUR
SHOW ME YOUR	BROTHER, HE'S YOUR SON. IF HE ASKED YOU TO WALK TO YOUR DEATH
PLAN. DON'T MAKE ME WAIT -- THE SEEDS WILL	YOU WOULD RUN. YOU LIVE FOR A SMILE; YOU ASK FOR A WORD. WHEN YOU
OPEN TOO LATE	SPEAK TO THE MAN YOU ARE HEARD. I WAS
HOW DID I COME TO THIS PLACE? PLEASE DON'T TURN A-WAY YOUR FACE. I'M CRYING FOR YOUR WORD HAVEN'T YOU HEARD? HAVEN'T YOU HEARD?	EMPTY -- NOW I'M FILLED. I WAS FALLOW. THEN HE TILLED. I WAS LONELY FOR A WORD. I WAS LONELY HE HEARD.

JOSEPH: Well, brother I can't decide if I have nothing to say, or if nothing needs saying
HYRUM: Everything needs saying, but there aren't any words
JOSEPH: *(Wordlessly takes Hyrum's hand)* I'm sorry
    (suddenly)
So chance has thrown us in here away from the Church.
HYRUM: There must be a purpose in it.
JOSEPH: Of course, everything's ordered Everything that happens in this world is the right thing Maybe not good Maybe not anything a man can ever like But it's right.
HYRUM: I gave up outguessing the Lord long ago, Joseph
JOSEPH: Yes, But He used to let me in on the secret now and

then

HYRUM: And now!?

JOSEPH: I'm worried.

HYRUM: So's Alex Macrae. He's convinced that Sidney was lying about the Danites.

JOSEPH: Alex Macrae. A good boy!

HYRUM: Boy! Not that much younger than you, little brother.

JOSEPH: Pain ages us all. He's already far older than anyone else born his same year. Everyone's getting too old too fast. I feel like I'll die of old age before I turn forty.

HYRUM: Me first.

JOSEPH: When can this people be at rest! When will the gentiles leave us alone!?

HYRUM: More to the point, when will the Saints start acting like Saints. I wonder how you put up with all the traitors in the Church.

JOSEPH: You work with what you're given, Hyrum. They just get a whiff of power and want to build their own kingdom. Thomas Marsh, John Corrill, William Phelps, Oliver -- Oliver, even Orson Hyde.

HYRUM: And Sidney.

JOSEPH: Maybe you didn't notice, but Sidney's in jail with us. Not out hobnobbing with apostates.

HYRUM: There are signs, Joseph. There have been for years.
(Joseph's silence seems like a rebuke)
I'm sorry, Joseph. I don't know. You tell me.

JOSEPH: Sidney is an able man.

HYRUM: Sidney is an able man.

JOSEPH: All right! Must the Church be led by incompetents because they have no ambition? Sidney's ambitious -- who isn't? Even Oliver. From the beginning he was with me. Visions, the translation, everything together. John the Baptist, Peter, James and John, priesthoods and powers. But he got ambitious and left.

HYRUM: Ambitious? He was hurt? He felt that Sidney had supplanted him.

JOSEPH: A strong man makes enemies.

HYRUM: Oliver wasn't the only one. Sidney has filled many places that didn't belong to him.

JOSEPH: *(Looks long and hard at Hyrum)* Sidney never filled a place that was full.

(Relenting)
The past is full of proof that God leads the Church but not yet my own life. Why am I here when my people need me? We've lost everything again, and again and again. I can see their fear and suffering, I can reach out to them, and my hands stop at the walls.
HYRUM: Sidney and Samson Avard were very close.
JOSEPH: Have a little mercy on me tonight, Hyrum.
HYRUM: They were Campbellite preachers together.
JOSEPH: So was Parley Pratt.
HYRUM: Joseph, the Danites weren't invented! Somebody convinced a lot of otherwise righteous Saints that the Prophet wanted them to burn down gentiles houses.
JOSEPH: Hyrum! I have to trust Sidney Rigdon or what is this Church? I'll die sooner or later. Probably sooner, if my enemies have their way. And what will happen to the Church if all the strong men are gone? I have loved and trusted again and again and how many are left? I can't decide which is more foolish. Giving a part of the Church to a man or giving him my whole heart. I pray about calling a man to office, and the Lord directs me. I pray about giving my heart and the Lord says give it to all men.
HYRUM: And many people love you, Joseph.
JOSEPH: Men like Alex. they love me as the Prophet. They love the spirit of God in me. Who loves a farm boy with no education? Who even knows he exists?
HYRUM: I do.
JOSEPH: How d'ya do. I believe we've met.
HYRUM: Believe so, Mister.
JOSEPH: Could be you recollect my name?
HYRUM: Slips my mind, Mister. Maybe you could tell me mine.
JOSEPH: Your name? Your name is comfort. Your name is silence when a man needs some good strong silence to shout into. Your name is home to a man who doesn't know where he can go. Your name is trust, no matter how long you have to wait.
HYRUM: Well You remember a lot of name from a man you haven't met but once and haven't seen in years. And your own name? Maybe you could refresh my memory.
JOSEPH: That's a hard question. I only use my brain but once a month on the second Thursday, and the light flickers

perilous close to going out altogether
> *(They laugh)*

There was once -- I was once called -- There was once somebody spoke to me in a voice I believed. He just called me Joseph.
HYRUM: Not so long as the name you remembered for me.
JOSEPH: Long enough, if I could only remember what it means. So many people have used it since then.
HYRUM: If you knew it once you can remember.
JOSEPH: If you can once name something then you can control it. Then it's not in control of you anymore. The whole name, the whole life of the thing, it's past and it's future. Then you can lay hold on it and it's yours.
HYRUM: Then name Sidney Rigdon for me!
JOSEPH: No.
HYRUM: Afraid
JOSEPH: No!
HYRUM: Angry?
JOSEPH: Do I have reason to be?
HYRUM: Plenty. Find out Sidney Rigdon's name, Joseph. Find out that it isn't your own.
JOSEPH: I'm tired. I want to sleep.
HYRUM: Good night.
> *(Joseph lays down and is asleep)*

SONG -- UNREMARKABLE THEY GROW

HYRUM:
UNREMARKABLE, THEY GROW.
NO LIGHT SHINING WHEN THEY SPEAK.
NO ONE KNOWING THAT THEY SEEK.
NO ONE SEEKING WHAT THEY KNOW.

JESUS, PLAYING IN THE DUST.
GALILEE GRIMED ON HIS FACE.
HIS CHAMELEON IN HIS RACE --
CHILD WITH GLORY HELD IN TRUST.

NOW, BESIDE US WHERE WE WALK
COMMON MEN ARE ALL WE SEE --
WHICH OF THEM MIGHT SET US FREE!

HIDE US WHEN THE HUNTERS STALK.

SIMPLE JOSEPH, FARMERS BOY.
JUST ANOTHER PIONEER.
HAD NOT TAUGHT WHAT HE COULD HEAR.
SOFT A NEW SONG WRUNG FROM JOY

SURE, WE KNEW THEM AS THEY WERE.
DID NOT WONDER WHAT THEY'D BE --
WHAT CAN COME FROM GALILEE?
UNTRAINED HANDS CAN NEVER CURE.

UNTRAINED HANDS CAN NEVER CURE.
BUT THEIR TOUCH CAN BE SO SWEET.
THEY CAN FIND THE FADING BEAT
OF A HEART. AND MAKE IT PURE.

Sheet Music for the Songs is available from the Publisher for $1.00 in a PDF format.

<u>DRAMATIC SCENE (with optional song): 2M • JOSEPH Smith & LYMAN Wight -- Act 2</u>
ABOUT THE CHARACTERS:
JOSEPH: The boy whom God trusted with the Restoration of His gospel, imperfect but always yearning to know the ways of truth. He is now in his 30s and feels that God has not spoken to him because of something he has done. But only now is he becoming aware of whom he can trust -- and who he cannot.
LYMAN: perceives the Gospel as truth, but is mired down by the ways and needs of 'man'. His head has been turned by Ridgon and Avard and others, almost to the point of declaring Joseph as a fallen prophet, when it is himself and the others he associates with who have fallen.

SONG -- ONLY (reprise)

JOSEPH: Is this my sojourn in the wilderness? I can bear it if I

feel like it has a good end.
ONLY FATHER SEES OUR HAND.
ONLY JESUS IS OUR FRIEND.
WE ARE SHEEP FOR HIM TO TEND.
ONLY HE WILL UNDERSTAND.
WE ARE MEN.
SONS OF GOD~
BUT STILL SONS.
STILL MEN.
NOT GODS.
BUT THERE IS A GOD WHO LOVES YOU.
WHEN OTHER MEN BETRAY YOU.
THERE IS A GOD WHO LOVES YOU.
THERE IS NOTHING MORE.
WHAT MORE DO I NEED?
WHEN DID THE MAN BECOME A PROPHET?
WHEN DID THE BOY BECOME A MAN?
WHO CAN TAKE A HOLD OF HEAVEN?
NOBODY CAN.

LYMAN: NOBODY CAN.

JOSEPH: Lyman - I'm sorry. I didn't know you were there.

LYMAN: I'm not. Ignore me - go ahead, talk to God, I want to see the technique.

JOSEPH: How did you get so much poison in you? Where's the Lyman Wight I used to know?

LYMAN: Where's mamma's good boy? He doesn't drown the cat. He doesn't write on the walls. He only does what mamma says to do.

JOSEPH: Lyman, whatever I've done, I'm sorry. Let me set it right.

LYMAN: Just what Sidney said.

JOSEPH: What did Sidney say?

LYMAN: Sidney said a lot of things. Damn all liars to the deepest, darkest cupboards in hell.

JOSEPH: Who has lied to you?

LYMAN: Thou sayest.

JOSEPH: I never lied to you, Lyman.

LYMAN: Oh, you're good! You've fooled thousands, even me. Me, Lyman Wight! Trusted you! Ha!

JOSEPH: Accuse me then, Lyman, when did I lie?

LYMAN: When didn't you?

JOSEPH: I didn't lie when I said an angel came to me. I didn't lie when I said Christ established this Church. I didn't lie when I said He called you, Lyman Wight, and commanded you to serve Him.

LYMAN: Serve whom? Christ, did you say? And what about the Danites, Mr. Smith?

JOSEPH: I never knew about the Danites.

LYMAN: You're lying!

JOSEPH: In the name of Christ, Lyman, I swear I never knew!

LYMAN: LIAR!

(Lyman attacks Joseph, and the struggle is fierce, with no words, only grunting, until Joseph gets the best of Lyman)

Let go of me!

JOSEPH: Why don't you believe me?

LYMAN: You're the Prophet! You're supposed to know what's going on!

JOSEPH: I can't see everything that happens.

LYMAN: This mattered!!

(Lyman tries to break free, Joseph adjusts the hold.)

JOSEPH: What do you think this Church is like? We aren't puppets with God pulling all the strings. He doesn't step in and save us from our stupidity, even when it matters. He teaches us as much as we're willing to learn, and then it's up to us!

LYMAN: You and Sidney, when I'm with you I believe you. When I'm alone I can see better.

JOSEPH: When I'm alone I can't see a thing

LYMAN: Let go of me.

JOSEPH: No.

LYMAN: Leave me alone.

JOSEPH: I don't want to leave you alone.

LYMAN: You already have.

JOSEPH: I didn't leave you.

LYMAN: You left us all! God's best friend, Joseph Smith.

JOSEPH: *(Letting go)* You never understood.

LYMAN: True. 'Till now.

JOSEPH: And what do you understand now? You men who trust in your own minds, your own arms, you don't want to be loved, you want to be followed.

LYMAN: Maybe we want both.

JOSEPH: God isn't God because he won all the wars! God is God because He loves every living soul!

LYMAN: You are so pious and perfect.

JOSEPH: You loved me once, Lyman.

LYMAN: Did I?

JOSEPH: But you coveted my power. If you'd only learn to love again you'd have that power

LYMAN: What are you offering?

JOSEPH: I'm offering you salvation, peace and joy and you see it as a back room deal.

LYMAN: You're offering me a chance to be under your thumb 'till death do us part.

JOSEPH: I'm offering you all I have and all I care about.

LYMAN: And I'm telling you I don't want it!

(Joseph stares at him intently for a moment, and then breaks out in a huge smile. He reaches out, and grabs Lyman in a huge bear hug, and laughs.)

JOSEPH: Thank you. Thank you, Lyman!

LYMAN: I beg your pardon, but if I just did you a favor it was an accident.

JOSEPH: You've finally made it clear to me.

LYMAN: Made what clear?

JOSEPH: Never mind.

LYMAN: I don't understand what's made you all dad-blamed happy all of a sudden.

JOSEPH: Do you want to understand?

LYMAN: Yes.

JOSEPH: Then why don't you?

LYMAN: Because you're talking in riddles, Joseph, so tell me what you're thanking me for and what I've made so clear to you.

JOSEPH: Why, who you are.

LYMAN: I'm nothing to you.

JOSEPH: Exactly. I never understood it until now.

(He starts to go.)

LYMAN: Where are you going?

JOSEPH: Upstairs.

LYMAN: You can't leave me now!

JOSEPH: Watch.

LYMAN: You owe me something!

JOSEPH: I've never borrowed anything from you in my life.

LYMAN: I've devoted my life to you!

JOSEPH: Too bad. You should have devoted it to Christ.

LYMAN: So I'm a nothing to you? You can just pretend I'm not here? You told me that you loved me, but you don't even know how.

JOSEPH: Oh, I know how to love, all right. I'm just learning how to let go, now. I was called to be a shepherd But I've been wasting half my time trying to gather up the wolves, and bring them into the flock. The wolves have got to go their own way.

LYMAN: Meaning me? You're calling me a wolf? I'm as much a part of this Church as anyone else!

JOSEPH: You can be, Lyman. You can. I'm prepared to love you more than you'll understand, Lyman, if you'll only repent and --

LYMAN: Repent! I haven't done one damn thing to repent of! I don't need anymore hypocrites in my life. Leave me alone.

JOSEPH: I don't have any other choice. But I'll still hear your cries in the hollow of your heart, and I'll long to let you out. Let me let you out.
 (Pause. No reaction)
 My people are suffering. I have no time for you, Lyman, unless you help them. I ask you to come back. But until you do, I have no time for you.

LYMAN: Are you telling me to leave?

JOSEPH: Yes.

LYMAN: And where should I go?

JOSEPH: Where you went a long time ago. Away from me.

LYMAN: Away from you, the only place I can go is up.
 (He laughs as he climbs the stairs but the laugh ends before the climb does.)

JOSEPH: *(kneels)* Where is the Pavilion that covers your hiding place?

Sheet music for the song is available from the publisher for $1.00 in PDF format.

Martyr In Waiting
a Short Play by *Carol Lynn Pearson*

ABOUT THE PLAY: Modern actors have gathered to stage a play about the sacrifices of the pioneers. They sometimes cannot equate what they are feeling from their experience in the play with their modern day feelings about life and history and sacrifice.

<u>DRAMATIC SCENE: 1M 2W • CALVIN, MARILYN & LINDA -- Act 2</u> *(Because of its 2:1 ratio of women to men, I included it.)*
ABOUT THE CHARACTERS:
CALVIN: *eager young actor convinced that there is nothing he can't tackle*
MARILYN: *an actor stuck on the physical things surrounding a role.*
LINDA: *kind of a newcomer*

(MARILYN gets to her knees down center and runs her fingers along the floor, as if through ashes. She picks up a small object and examines it.)
MARILYN: Susan's hair brush -- not a bristle left.
(Hearing a noise, she turns, startled)
Who's there?
CALVIN: Don't be frightened
(Coming downstage)
MARILYN: *(Rising)* Oh, Brother Allen, I couldn't see you.
CALVIN: You can't go wandering around out here at night.
MARILYN: They wouldn't come back here. My house is in ashes. What more could they do? You know what I was thinking as I watched the house burn? The baby was crying and Robert was pulling at my skirt. I just stood there and watched the flames. It was like losing Tom all over again. He built this house.
CALVIN: Tom was a fine man.
MARILYN: Every morning he'd get up at five and work on the house until noon -- then go and help build the temple. He

wanted us to have one of the finest houses in Nauvoo.

CALVIN: It was. Tom was a good craftsman.

MARILYN: *(Crosses left to beside chair)* All the hours he put on those bookshelves. All the carving. And polishing. "We'll never use all those bookshelves, Tom, not in a hundred years," I said. But he'd go right on building and carving. "Oh yes, we will," he'd say. "This is our home forever, and my children are going to own a whole library full of books -- right here in our own house." He sent me our seventh book from England while he was on his mission ., just before he died of the fever. They're gone now -- all of them.

CALVIN: We'd better be
   (Crosses down to her level)

MARILYN: *(Building in intensity)* I tried to run back in while it was burning, but they wouldn't let me. I wanted to get something for the children -- something of their father. His letters. He wrote such beautiful letters so strong.
   (On the verge of tears)
   I wanted the children to have his words -- his strength.

CALVIN: *(Low and intense)* Damn them! Damn all of them!

MARILYN: I shouldn't have gone on like that. I'm not bitter -- really. The Lord is just -- proving us.
   (LINDA runs into the scene from right.)

LINDA: Daniel, come quick! They're stealing the oxen!

CALVIN: The oxen?

LINDA: And the horses! Hurry!

CALVIN: *(Running out door upper right)* Get in the house, both of you. And lock the doors.
   (He re-enters, crosses down by PAUL.)

LINDA: *(Putting her shawl around ELIZABETH)* Elizabeth, you'll catch your death of cold.

MARILYN: Are the children all right?

LINDA: They're fine. If they take the animals we'll never make it west.

MARILYN: We'll make it -- if we have to walk.

LINDA: A messenger from President Young just came. We can't stay until spring.

MARILYN: *(Whirls to face LINDA)* But they promised!

LINDA: Promises! What do promises mean to a hate-filled mob! We're going now -- in the dead of winter. Hurry, Elizabeth.

(Holds out hand to MARILYN. As they start to leave. MARILYN leans down and picks up something from the ground.)
MARILYN: Robert's jackknife.
LINDA: Hurry!
(They exit door left.)

Matters of the Heart
A Play by *Thom Duncan*

ABOUT THE PLAY: A heart-wrenching and inspired look at a Stake President's family who's youngest son returns early from a Full-time LDS Mission. We come to know the Mother, The Father and the Son -- we know them because we are them.

<u>DRAMATIC MONOLOGUE:1M • Robert M. BAINES -- Act 1 Scene One</u>
ABOUT THE CHARACTER:
BAINES: *nearly 60, a newly appointed Stake President. He is speaking to his Wife of many years.*

BAINES: Oh, I love all my sons -- you know that. But Paul was always special to me -- from the day he was born. Just like Israel and Joseph. I remember the day you brought him home. You had him on the basinet, and he rolled over onto his stomach, lifted his head and looked around through squinty eyes. It was in that split second -- that frozen moment of time -- that I saw the entire course of Paul's life stretching out before him. I knew then that, in the face of the unknown, Paul would not shrink but would lift up his head and face life straight on -- eyes squinty, perhaps, but he would face it. And he was always that way -- all through school. If a problem was too tough, he would bite his lip and tackle it until he mastered it. Do you remember how he spent days patiently trying to tie his shoe? Never seeming to get frustrated, or discouraged. None of the other boys were like that. That's what makes it so difficult to accept -- Paul's coming home. I get the feeling that he's ... running away from something. And I can't understand that.

<u>DRAMATIC SCENE:1M 1W • Robert M. BAINES & ALICE</u>

Baines -- Act 1 Scene One

ABOUT THE CHARACTER:

BAINES: nearly 60, a newly appointed Stake President. He toes the line, he does what he thinks God wants him to do, and he is right -- mostly.

ALICE: his wife, aged 58, and clearly devoted to him and their mission of raising a son and living a life that can be considered as one devoted to God. She understands her husband -- and her son. She is, after all, a mother.

> *BAINES is standing at the door. He turns. ALICE comes to him. He takes her in his arms. BAINES and ALICE break their embrace. BAINES goes to window, looks out)*

BAINES: He's just going through a rebellious stage. That's all. He's been trained well. He'll go out, cool off, then come back and apologize. After a few days, he'll probably ask to finish out his mission.

ALICE: "He's been trained well." You make him sound like a circus animal.

BAINES: I was simply paraphrasing scripture: "Train up a child in the path to follow, and he will not depart therefrom."

ALICE: Kelly Thorenson did. He had good parents.

BAINES: That's an isolated case --

ALICE: Lehi had two sons who never came back.

BAINES: Yes ...

ALICE: Elohim had a rebellious son.

BAINES: *(Somewhat cuttingly)* Alice, are you siding with him and his radical ideas?

ALICE: What's so radical about a son wanting a father to love him?

BAINES: My love for him is not the issue here. He obviously feels he's been coerced into going on his mission.

ALICE: Hasn't he?

BAINES: No. Encouraged perhaps. I feel badly that he perceives that as coercion.
   (As if he can't believe it)
You sound as though you're condoning his actions.

ALICE: I'm not condoning anything.
   (Pause)

I just think I know how he feels.

BAINES: What do you mean?

ALICE: *(After a long pause)* Robert, it's -- very difficult living in the shadow of a great man.

BAINES: *(Slowly, pained)* You, too?

ALICE: Don't think I don't support you ...

BAINES: I can't very well ask to be released simply because my family finds it difficult to live with me.

ALICE: And I'm not asking you to.

BAINES: I know. This thing with Paul has me so upset, I don't know what I'm saying anymore....

ALICE: We'll figure Paul out together.

BAINES: Yes, we will. That's really the only way, isn't it?
(Pause)
So what are your thoughts? What is Paul's problem?

ALICE: I think it's exactly what he say it is. He doesn't feel he can handle the responsibility.

BAINES: But remember what he said when I asked him where he was going? He said, "Wherever I want to." And then there's that passage in his journal. It seems to me he's making some stand for independence.

ALICE: That, too.

BAINES: Then I'm worried. Because the independent thinker has no place in the Church. "Let thy will be done," the scripture says. Not ours. The whole plan of the Church is to subjugate our own egos to the Lord's. If Paul can't do that, then he's in for a difficult time the rest of his life.... I wish President Andrews would call back.

ALICE: You should have let Paul tell you at his convenience.

BAINES: So you're saying that I made my own son leave this house? As if I had stood at the door and said, "Get out of here!"

ALICE: Don't be so hard on yourself. I'm sure I'm part of the problem, too.

BAINES: You -- ?

ALICE: And his brothers. We're all a family. We're all responsible to some degree for whatever's happening to Paul. He's zeroed in on you because you're the most visible.

BAINES: Alice, I don't want to lose him. I love him.

ALICE: Then when he comes back, why don't you tell him that?

BAINES: He knows I love him.

ALICE: Does he?

BAINES: It should be quite evident, I would think, after all these years. I've spent quality time with him. I've had personal interviews with him. We've played handball together. Exactly what I've done with all the other boys.

ALICE: But Paul is not like the other boys. We've already established that. He needs to be treated differently. You need to let him be himself, right or wrong.

BAINES: He's only twenty years old, Alice, and obviously is not capable of making correct choices.

ALICE: Paul is not some hardened criminal you're letting loose on society. He's a highly intelligent, spiritual young man who's going through some real emotional problems right now.

BAINES: Why do I feel like it's you and him versus the mean ogre of a dad?

ALICE: I'm not taking sides. I can't take sides where matters of the heart are concerned. I love you both. I want you both to be happy, but each in your own way. And you're not a mean ogre. I don't think Paul would feel that way, either. You're a little stubborn around the edges, maybe ...

BAINES: *(After a pause)* You know what I'd like, Alice? It's strange, because I haven't thought this for many years -- at least since my mission. I wish that ... somehow ... I could just take everything that's in my heart and soul, everything I know and feel about this glorious Church and transfer it wholesale into Paul. If he could only see the great vision of this work as I do there'd be no problem, no conflict between us.

ALICE: And no growth.

Move On!
A Play with music by *Carol Lynn Pearson*

ABOUT THE PLAY: MOVE ON! is a play of mostly monologues and some scenes that explore the Pioneer Trek, in handcart or wagon -- or on foot -- through the actual journal entries of those pioneers. The author has woven them together to make a powerful and sometimes humorous tale -- not really a story -- but a journey on stage through the lives of the characters of the play.

DRAMATIC MONOLOGUE:1M • BRIGHAM Young ABOUT THE CHARACTER:
BRIGHAM YOUNG: The current Prophet and leader of the Church. A motivation speech to get people to move. He must lead, guide and direct -- through his example. Something at which he was very good.

BRIGHAM): "We are going to try and save ourselves, and when we come to understanding we will then be counted worthy to possess Zion, even the Centre stake of Zion. It is true this is the land of Zion; but we are not prepared to go and establish the Centre Stake of Zion. The Lord tried this in the first place. He called the people together to the place where the New Jerusalem and where the great temple will be built, and where He will prepare for the City of Enoch ... finally they were driven into the mountains, and here we are. Now, it is for you and me to prepare to return back again. We are not prepared to do this now, but we are here to learn until we are of one heart and of one mind in the things of this life ... Are their eyes single to the building up of the kingdom of God? No, they are single to the building up of themselves.

When will Zion be redeemed? When will the Savior make his appearance in the midst of his people? Just as soon as the Latter-day Saints are ready and prepared to return to Independence, Jackson County, in the State of Missouri, North America, just as soon will the voice of the Lord be heard. 'Arise now, Israel, and make your way to the Center Stake of Zion.'

SERIO-COMIC MONOLOGUE:1W • IRENE
ABOUT THE CHARACTER:
IRENE: one of the few recurring characters in the play, one that has a name, writes a letter to her sister and shares it with the audience. In that sharing it must be personalized and full of the subtext of its words. It is not a recitation but a re-enactement.

IRENE: "Camp of Israel, Sept. 19, 1846. Dear Sister, In the wilds of North America is the residence of your affectionate sister. Not unhappy and suffering, no, far from it, not none of our family. There is nothing that would induce me to leave the company of the saints of God. We traveled until we came to Council Bluffs on the Missouri River (you can find it on the map). There we found the camp of Israel waiting for a boat to be built to carry us across the river. Here we camped two weeks, then the boat was ready. All crossed as fast as possible, came on twenty miles this side of the river, and stopped a while, finally to stay here this winter, and let those that are ahead break the way and we start early in the spring. They consented to it, went to work. Cut grass and made such big stacks of hay as I never thought of, for the cattle, building log cabins for their families. Some split the logs. Francis split his. They make boards and shingles here by hand. They brought saws and almost everything else. They brought a carding machine. I think they will need it, there is seven hundred sheep in one drove that is church property, there is lots of fat cattle killed, one or two every day this six weeks. We have some every week, Francis and Thales got a lot of honey the other day equal to Daniels, the warm biscuit and honey is not so mean. Do not worry about us, I think we shall get along with as little trouble as other people that live in painted houses with carpet floors.

The Indians are very plenty here. They are here begging every week. Sometimes they steal a tin cup or garment if it lies in their way. Brigham Young has made a treaty with them. They are to have our houses and all the improvements when we leave. We found one tribe that had several that had been baptized by Joseph. They would say 'me Mormon.'

Direct your letters to Huntsuckers post office, Atchison County, Missouri. Love from your affectionate sister."

COMIC MONOLOGUE: 1M • MAN
ABOUT THE CHARACTER:

MAN 1: His name is unimportant. His sentiment is vital. He is a representative of all who traveled in the name of God across a wilderness. He has a passion. These words must become his own, not just something he read.

MAN 1: *(Reading from a newspaper, laughing occasionally, as if he is enjoying it immensely)* "Warsaw Signal, December 31, 1845. The best joke of the season was played off, last week, by the Saints, on the United States deputy Marshall for Illinois. It appears that Brigham Young and other Saints were indicted at the last term of the United States Circuit Court at Springfield, for Bogus making. On Tuesday of last week, the Deputy Marshall, accompanied by eight of the Hancock Guard, and Mr. Benson of Augusta, (who went along to point out Brigham) started from Carthage for the Holy City. On arriving they went to the Temple, where the Saints were assembled, and soon Mr. Benson pointed out Brigham, accompanied by some ladies, in the act of getting into a carriage. The Marshall immediately walked up and arrested him.

The Saints, learning what had been done, assembled around the prisoner and swore that he should not be taken out of town. The Marshall and his posse were, however, determined and declared if any effort was made to rescue him they would shoot Brigham the first man. After considerable bluster, the Saints began to cool off and the prisoner was taken to the tavern. The Saints now began to show long faces and seemed very much affected.

As the Officer and his posse left with their charge they broke out in such strains as these: "Farewell, Brother Brigham. We hope you soon will return." "May the Lord bless you, Brother Brigham, and grant you safe deliverance." On arriving at Carthage, the prisoner was put under a sufficient guard and was carefully watched.

Some time after his arrival, G. W. Thatcher, Esq., went in to see him. Soon he returned with a very knowing look, and affirmed that there was no Brigham Young there, and the prisoner was an entirely different personage. An investigation was gone into and sure enough it turned out that the Saints had, by putting the cloak and cap of the apostle on the man who resembled him in figure and appearance, first deceived Mr. Benson, and then by planning well their part, had prevented any suspicion from arising in the minds of nay of the company that they had got the wrong pig by the ear. The Marshall, on learning that he had been hoaxed, released the prisoner and now says the Saints may "have his hat." The United States Marshall, after being sadly humbugged in Nauvoo, returned to the city to get the real Brigham, but it was no good. Of course Brigham could not be found."

DRAMATIC MONOLOGUE:1M • MAN
ABOUT THE CHARACTER:
MAN 6: He is a man, like any of the rest of us. His experience speaks to us of the pain and sorrow that comes with sacrifice. It may be short, but it should not be quick. It also should not be over-indulged in. This is a moment of the recounting of loss. These are his words, speak them with respect.

MAN 6: "Saturday, May 9th, 1846. I was sent for and informed that my little son Hirum was dying. I returned immediately home and found the poor little afflicted child in the last agonies of death. He died in my arms about 4 o'clock. This was the second child which I had lost, both dying in my arms. He died with the whooping cough and black canker. He had worn down ever since he first took it. My wife is yet unable to go about, and little Hosea, my only son now, is wearing down with the same complaint, and what will be the end thereof? We are truly desolate and afflicted, and entirely destitute of anything even to eat, much less to nourish the sick, and just able to go about myself. Arrangements made to bury him this evening."

DRAMATIC MONOLOGUE:1W • WOMAN 4
ABOUT THE CHARACTER:
WOMAN 4: another woman who represents many others on the trek West. She has settled in the Salt Lake Valley and now her husband is called away. She speaks of that thing that is only so little demanded of the modern Saint -- sacrifice.

WOMAN 4: "In 1876 William was called to go and help settle Arizona and given six months to get ready in ... It was cruel it seemed to me ... but we were called, and there was no other way, so we began to make preparations ... We got only $1,200.00 for our home in town. A person has to take what he can get when he has to move. We left our home November 19th ... My baby was just 3 months old to the day and was quite sick.
I did all I could with medicine, and also with faith. My prayers did not seem to be heard, but several times a day I went away from my wagon and in secret prayed for my child, had him administered to often but there seemed to be no faith. I was sad indeed, away from home and kindred and my husband away. For a long time I did not blow the candle out at night. On the morning of July 6th, 1878, I was so deep in sorrow it seemed I could not bear it any longer. I went out in some brush to pray and asked my Father in Heaven to take him from his suffering, I felt I could not endure it longer. The prayer was simple, but from the heart. I went to him, he breathed a few times, then passed away so

sweetly. With my own hands I made his little clothes, dressed him, fixed some paint and painted his coffin ... The next day we took our beloved little treasure to the nearest town--St. Joseph--and buried him.

The Plan
A Play by *Eric Samuelsen*

ABOUT THE PLAY: A play made up of six similarly themed short plays that take us from before the Creation through some of the most notable and memorable passages of the Old Testament, allowing us to meet important players as they relate to The Plan Of Salvation.

DRAMATIC MONOLOGUE:1W • RUTH (20s)
ABOUT THE CHARACTER:
RUTH: a woman who trusts in God, knows what He wants and is willing to do it. She is young, He is… older.

RUTH: He's still asleep. I could just leave. I don't think anyone saw me come in and if I'm very quiet I could slip out and no one would know I was here. Yes. Yes.
(She starts to get up.)
No. Don't lose your nerve, you're just scared. Naomi said it was okay. Besides, where would I go? Back to Naomi? She'll ask what happened, and I'll have to tell her what a coward I am. She won't despise me, I don't think. She never has, even when Mahlon married me, which I know disappointed her, her son with a Moabite, rejecting his own people and God, but no, never a word, she's been my great friend throughout. Oh! He's stirring! I don't like this! Leave! Run!
(She starts to get up.)
Calm yourself. Calm down.
(She stands, irresolute.)
What's the worst that could happen? He could misunderstand. He could laugh at me. Or he could kick me out and tell us we can't glean from his fields anymore. Or…
(An appalling possibility.)
He could understand all too well. I'm here, at his bedside, brazen like a harlot. He's a man, after all. He could… do as men do. Take his pleasure. And what could I do but

consent? I am here, after all. I chose to sneak into his bedchamber, lay myself down, uncover his feet. Pretty much just inviting him to…
(Starts to go.)
This was foolishness. I trust Naomi, she knows the customs here. But customs are just customs, and men have their desires. And if the worst should happen, I'm no blushing virgin. I was married. But a widow is respectable, a widow can hold her head up. I'm a stranger, but I am an honorable woman, I am no strumpet. Some things are just wrong.
(Firmly preparing to leave.)
I must leave, I have no choice. And I suppose that probably means leaving Naomi too, and returning, as Orpah did, home, to my own land and people. If my choices are poverty or dishonor, I know which I choose. Orpah will take me in.
(Considers it.)
Orpah. My sister. Who left poor Naomi to grieve alone, after losing her husband, losing two sons. After vowing to stay with her. That's who I want to be? Another Orpah?
(She sits.)
And what reason do I have to distrust Naomi? Or distrust the family of Elimalech? These are good people, caring and kind, and they've taught me so much, about the lovingkindness of Yahweh. Naomi said this was a right and proper act, though that seems quite impossible, and even terribly dangerous. But Naomi knows their ways. Besides…
(She looks down at BOAZ, still sleeping.)
Does he really seem so frightening? When he told his servants to let us glean his barley, he spoke so softly and kindly. Perhaps he is different from other men. Maybe this will be all right.
(BOAZ stirs again.)
Oh! He's waking! Pretend to be asleep!
(She lays quickly down and feigns sleep.)

DRAMATIC MONOLOGUE:1M • BOAZ (30s)
ABOUT THE CHARACTER:
BOAZ: A landowner, quite wealthy and very righteous. He is surprised to find a woman in his bedchamber. It makes him uneasy.

(BOAZ wakes. Yawns, stretches. He sees RUTH sleeping.)

BOAZ: What in the world?
(He looks her over.)
She shouldn't be here.
(Gently shakes her shoulder.)
Miss? Miss?
(RUTH continues to pretend she's asleep.)
Of all the strange situations… Do I know her?
(Looks her over carefully.)
I saw her gleaning from my fields. The Moabite. Daughter-in-law to the one who was gone and returned, Naomi. Yes, I remember, she's the one. We talked briefly, she spoke so softly and well. And the others wanted to make fun of her accent, and her looks and ways, but that wasn't right, she's a loyal friend to her mother-in-law and they ought to have respected that. But what is she doing here? Could she have misunderstood? Could she have thought I was inviting her to be with me, as a woman and a man, together? Does she really think so little of me, to think I'd want her that way? A poor woman giving herself to me, a man of means?
(Looks her over again.)
But wait. Naomi, the one who left. The one she takes care of. She's kin to me, is she not? Distant kin, perhaps, but we share… an uncle, perhaps? Are we in someway cousins? So is this about my obligation to her?
(A little angry.)
So this is a demand, is it? An insolent ultimatum. The arrogance of it: support me, your kinswoman, or else. Or else what? What will she do to me, who can she turn to? I'll show her how power works in Israel.
(Shakes her again.)
Wake up!
(RUTH sits up, frightened, and turns away from him. He turns away from her as well.)
She certainly doesn't look insolent.

<u>*DRAMATIC SCENE: 1M 1W • LUCIFER, GAIA (16-22)*</u>
ABOUT THE CHARACTERS:
LUCIFER: the being who, through his own choice, became Satan. A complex and jealous and doubting individual. But he does have an admirable determination to do what he thinks is right. Should appear young in age.
GAIA: the being who became Eve, our earthly Mother. Trusting and spiritual; knows things through discernment that most others cannot get a sense of. Should appear almost too young in age.

> *(A non-descript, pre-existence type of location. LUCIFER and GAIA have been talking and it all culminates in this scene. Remember this is a fantasy, an invention; not history.)*

LUCIFER: Are you going to tell me to stop talking to people?
GAIA: I'll be talking to them afterwards.
LUCIFER: Then do me a favor. Tell HIM something for me. Tell HIM I know.
GAIA: What do you know?
LUCIFER: What HIS was like. HIS probation. I've seen it.
> *(Shocked pause.)*
GAIA: That's not possible.
LUCIFER: Hey, you said I was bright.
GAIA: Show me.
LUCIFER: You sure?
GAIA: Show me!
LUCIFER: HE was nothing special. I figured, you know, HE was probably a king, or an artist, or someone really important. But no. See for yourself.
> *(LUCIFER steps back. GAIA looks.)*
He's twenty, MOTHER was sixteen. They have two children. They sleep on some straw on a dirt floor. They eat with wooden forks. They're no one. They have nothing.
GAIA: That's FATHER.
LUCIFER: There HE is. This is as old as HE ever got. He married at seventeen, normal in that day. These guys came

by. They had some dispute with HIS master, and they took it out on his slaves. There.
(GAIA recoils from the view in utter horror.)
HE fought back as best HE could. But you can see. It was over pretty quickly.

GAIA: Why would you show me this?

LUCIFER: To show you how hypocritical this all is! Look at HIM? HE did nothing! HE was nobody! Someone to be slaughtered.

GAIA: HE loved HER. Look how HE fought for HER.

LUCIFER: Yes, HE loved! But look at HIM. Worked half to death, with nothing to show for it. How could HE make any choices at all? How was HE judged? HE's sending us down as a test? To think, to grow, to learn? Well, what did HE ever learn? How was HE really human?

GAIA: And you don't see that?

LUCIFER: I see a peasant being bludgeoned to death.

GAIA: No! A MAN, in love. A MAN who cared for his family! Powerless and weak, perhaps, but look at the choices HE made nonetheless!

LUCIFER: I see an animal slaughtered. And I don't think it's fair for me to have to live up to some higher standard than that.

GAIA: Is that all you can see? How unfair things are to you?

LUCIFER: Fair's fair, and HE's not being fair. And I'm telling everyone, and some already believe me.

GAIA: So it's true. When Yahweh told me--.

LUCIFER: Yahweh, what did he say about me?

GAIA: He said there was a role in the plan for you. An important role, a necessary role. But a terrible one. And you had to choose it, and you could decide not to, but…
(She stops.)

LUCIFER: What? I could decide not to, but what?

GAIA: But that you probably wouldn't.

LUCIFER: Well. Now I am intrigued. What great role is this?

GAIA: The tempter. The destroyer. The opposition.

LUCIFER: That's what they've ordained for me?

GAIA: It's not ordained! It's not something HE can ordain! But they see the way you're heading, and it makes… some sense.

LUCIFER: So it looks like I'll be in the garden with you after all.

GAIA: You don't have to! This is still something you can decide not to do!
LUCIFER: Hey, this is great, for once, they're taking me seriously.
GAIA: Lucifer, you've seen Father's mortality! When you look at that life, that short, painful, loving life, you feel no compassion?
LUCIFER: I feel nothing but contempt. And you still think HE's great, don't you?
GAIA: More than ever.
LUCIFER: What a sentimental weakling you are.
GAIA: And I had no idea you'd fallen so far.
LUCIFER: Fallen? You just said it, I'm essential! I'm needed!
GAIA: I'm so sorry, Lucifer.
LUCIFER: Hey, you tell 'em from me. I'll still go! If they want me to, I'll go. But on my terms!
GAIA: Goodbye.
(She exits leaving LUCIFER to ponder his greatness.)

DRAMATIC SCENE:1M 1W • JACOB, LEAH (19 & 26)
ABOUT THE CHARACTERS:
JACOB: has grown up with Yahweh in his life, home, society. The Gospel is in its third generation with him and he takes it very seriously.
LEAH: the eldest daughter and sister to Rachael, the woman Jacob really wants to marry. She is plain but strong and courageous. Resolute.

(They are in a tent.)
JACOB: Two partners, standing together, worshipping Yahweh as independent equals.
LEAH: And then it lasts! It doesn't just end when we die, we don't face judgement alone! I heard what you said, night after night, and it burned, it burned in my soul! That's what I want. That's what my father wants for me. For both his daughters. And there isn't anybody else, it's got to be with you. No else gets it.

JACOB: I've tried to tell other people, but you're right. Their minds are closed. Especially... guys.

LEAH: So that's why the seven years.

JACOB: So we can have time, just the two of us.

LEAH: So that I have a chance! You love Rachel, I know that. But I'm... I'm a person too. Just because she's cuter and smaller and... pretty. And I know I'm not. It's okay. It's actually not okay, it stinks, but... I deserve a chance. To stand before Yahweh with someone who thinks of me as... a co-equal, a mate. I deserve that.

JACOB: You could have all that. With someone else. It's your father's job, to make a good match for you.

LEAH: No. It had to be you.

JACOB: Good man are rare, that's true. But your father's a wealthy man, he could search far and wide.

LEAH: Looking for what?

JACOB: A decent man, a good husband.
(Stops to consider.)
Who worships Yahweh.

LEAH: That's it, that's the problem. You told us about Abraham's promise. "As numerous as grains of sand on a beach." I believe that, I think it's possible, the ideas your grandfather taught will spread. But we're at the beginning of that chain. Who else is there today who understands?

JACOB: No one.

LEAH: No. So here you are. I can settle for a marriage that's maybe a tiny baby step above slavery, or I can stay single all my life. Or, there's you. The one truly eligible bachelor in the world. Promised to my sister, and deeply in love with her.

JACOB: So your Dad tricked me.

LEAH: Runs in the family, soup boy.

JACOB: Fair enough.

LEAH: My father bought us some time. Bought me some time. A chance to be together, to form a relationship. And bought you some time to actually see me, as me, as a person. And maybe even...

JACOB: Fall in love.

LEAH: Something like that.

JACOB: But after seven years, Rachel will also be my wife.

LEAH: And I'll have to share my marriage with Rachel. And I'm willing to do that, I really am. All I want is a chance.

(Pause.)
So what do you say?
JACOB: I… don't mean to hurt you. But I'm still in love with Rachel.
LEAH: And you're not in love with me.
JACOB: No. And that's what makes the whole thing possible, the whole partnership Yahweh wants us to have. And I'm not unwilling to, you know, give this a try. I do see you as a person, Leah, I do admire you and I see your good qualities. But I'm in love with someone else.
LEAH: So what is it? Love. Something you fall into? Like falling off a cliff, or falling in a lake?
JACOB: Love is the key.
LEAH: Doesn't make sense. Some force you can't control? It's like saying, hey, never mind all that talk about sin, the key to salvation is who trips the fewest times. Sorry, you're sort of clumsy, to Gehenna with you.
JACOB: But that *is* what happens. The first moment I saw Rachel, I knew, love at first sight.
LEAH: Predestinate, huh? Ordained by God?
JACOB: But… that's how it feels.
LEAH: So. I know that feeling. I've been in love. With someone else, not you.
JACOB: Your father refused him?
LEAH: I refused him. He worshipped Dagon. The fish god? You don't even want to know their worship rites, plus there was the human sacrifice angle, plus plus plus.
JACOB: Oh.
LEAH: Not a bad man. Not a good vision.
JACOB: But you loved him.
LEAH: I thought so.
JACOB: All I know is how I feel. That first moment, I saw her, I barely even knew what I was doing, I walked up to her, and I took her face in my hands, and I kissed her. I hadn't even told her my name. Like I was holding the rarest, most precious, most delicate gift in the world in my arms.
LEAH: A gift from Yahweh.
JACOB: Yes!
LEAH: So He's given us another gift, you and I. One that might be even more precious.
JACOB: More precious than love?

LEAH: Time. And a chance.
JACOB: And what of our children?
LEAH: What about them?
JACOB: Will I favor Rachel over you? How can I not? Will I favor her children over yours?
LEAH: Our children!
JACOB: But I'll know. There's my son by Rachel, there's my son by Leah. I don't think I can do this.
LEAH: We have seven years to make it work for us.
JACOB: I don't know… if I can.
LEAH: Can't we at least try?
JACOB: I don't know. I've already served seven years, you know. And they seemed like no time at all, because of Rachel, because of my love for her. Now, seven more years?
LEAH: Try. Or leave. Those are your choices.
JACOB: This isn't fair to you.
LEAH: No it isn't. And I know that the day you marry her too will hurt worse than anything I've ever experienced. At least I'm prepared.
JACOB: I'm sorry about that too.
LEAH: But I'm willing. Pain and all, I'll risk it.
JACOB: Let's be married, then.
(With a great breath, LEAH sighs in relief.)
LEAH: All right.
(She embraces him. He holds her. But on his face we read his fear.

Zion BookWorks

Planemaker
A Musical Play by *Marvin Payne and Guy Randle*

ABOUT THE PLAY: This is the magical story of a boy who dreamed he could fly -- his childhood nickname was, after all, The Planemaker -- and then, eventually did. Through the eyes of youth, LUCAS Lightbrow, who has become an old man, has his dreams rekindled by the fire of his grandson, Merwin. LUCAS has lost everything but his son and grandson. He is lonely and solitary -- and old. Merwin ignites memories long dormant and they build a plane together. This plane, shared with his grandson, will now become the vehicle that reunites him with his beloved Amy Fletcher -- the embodiment of 'yellow' in Lucas' life -- Merwin's grandmother. As they fly away and travel through space, time, dimensions, galaxies, whatever; they become -- together -- a star, a sun. Something eternal and blessed.

SERIO-COMIC MONOLOG: 1M (orW) Monologuist (any age)
ABOUT THE CHARACTER:
MONOLOGUIST: The storyteller and interpreter of dreams. He becomes whom he is talking about, gets involved in the story as persons, characters, and we see more clearly because we see it all through him.

> *The space is a stage, open and inviting, with no thoughts in it yet until we bring them and add them to the words that the monologist gives us. We are, after all, world-building.*

MONOLOGUIST: The plane streams steadily on and when at last he awakes in the greying east, he finds himself far out over some green ocean. He thinks about Merwin. He thinks about home. He thinks it was time he was getting back. So, in his mind he banks the plane to starboard and sails off for home. He's carefully rehearsing all the fantastic things he'll tell Merwin when suddenly, he realizes that the plane never banked at all back there... and it's shooting on ahead. That scares him a little. He tries banking to port. No luck. He tries every way except straight ahead but the plane seems to be under another power. That scares him alot.

The sky slowly lightens and the morning sun breaks on the horizon. Then is scares him like crazy to sense that as the sun climbs higher and higher from the rim of the world...the nose of his plane is rising exactly with it. Like it's being drawn magnetically, irresistibly, into the sun. Higher he climbs ...up through billowing banks of clouds ...whistling toward the end of air... locked on a course for the sun itself. He looks back and moans... then breaks up and out through the final edge of the earth's bright glow and off through clear, sharp space.

(Music should end here)

As he shoots past the cool orb of the moon he gives himself up for dead. But somehow he knows that he isn't. He zooms in on what , at first, looked like a star but now becomes the fuzzed edge of Venus. And he gives himself up for dead -- but he still isn't. But he wishes he was! Rocketing past, he flies faster on, drawn like a missle to the sun! It gets bigger and brighter and fiercer and stronger...and he's about to give himself up for dead ...but he's getting discouraged with that.

Then he whips around Mercury and suddenly half the sky is solid sun! He's about decided he'll just have to live through it all...when right behind him he hears a screech and a wrenching groan... And he gives himself up for dead.

The whole plane begins to shudder. He looks around in a flat panic to see the struts and rods and wires glowing bright, right on the point of melting. Achingly, slowly the broad wings and the tall tailpiece begin to bend out behind, until the stricken dream-plane explodes into a trillion tiny drips and pieces and sweeps away behind the doomed old man who's screaming head over heels into... into... into yellow. Into bright, fat, yellow!

So this is the place! Why didn't I see it coming? The place he once knew in his mind and forgot ...where blank space dissolves into warm rolling waves.

(HE laughs out loud)

They crash over his tumbling body giving him strength...washing away his fear and trembling. He spreads out his arms and points his toes and tears like an arrow on into the heart of the sun, his long white beard trailing behind him. In all that rich warm yellow he remembers his Amy and he almost expects her to reach out from nowhere and take his

hand -- But then the yellow begins to thin, like he's moving too fast and the yellow itself is on fire and flaming into white.
And easily into white passes Lucas Lightbrow.
And the white passes fiercely into him, tearing the years from behind his eyes. And now he sees a million colors in the white and each one sings a deep song of its own.
 (HE laughs loudly again)
And Lucas flashes a million colors back. Then bashes out the other side of the sun and blazes through heaven like a bright new star. Double bright, because the brightness of Lucas Lightbrow and the brightness of Amy Fletcher are now one fiercely everlasting brightness! Like a comet they sail, hand in hand, through heavens measured in millions of light-years. And they frighten dogs and delight children and excite lovers across a thousand galaxies. Until at last, they come to rest in deep, deep space above a dark and empty world -- A world where life has never been.
And there they stay.

Reunion
A Play by *Thomas F. Rogers*

ABOUT THE PLAY: With a father dying of cancer (ARTHUR) and a son about to leave on his mission (BILLY), the family gathers -- to do what? Say good bye to the son, say goodbye to the father (before he tells them he's even sick), argue again about their own beliefs or lack of them. The three oldest children, now living away from home, have come together to celebrate the missionary farewell of their youngest brother Billy. They are also concerned about their father Arthur who, they discover, is dying of cancer. Despite their desire for an agreeable reunion, the older children's misfortunes, grievances and mutual antagonisms soon rise to the surface: Chris, an airline stewardess, maintains a clandestine liaison with her pretended fiancé, a married man. Wayne, a school teacher, who did not complete his mission, is sour about people in the Church and ready to abandon his career and family. Jerold, a prosperous broker and active churchman, resents the others' "liberality" but has alienated his own teenage son, who recently left home. While fretting over the many surface manifestations that all is not right in their children's lives, Arthur's wife Mildred tries to put a pleasant face on things. In turn, Arthur maintains a stoic and tolerant facade. Wayne and Jerold finally square off with a classic debate that touches upon practically every area of controversy that was ever argued between Mormons. This triggers Arthur's reminiscence about his earlier days as a seminary teacher, an oil stock fraud, his brother Fred's consequent suicide, and even his first son Larry's death in Vietnam--all somehow related. Disillusioned by the cumulative spirit of contention and incrimination, Billy shocks the others, in the presence of the home teachers by threatening not to go on his mission. The family's feelings of alienation and despair reach a turning point only after Arthur breaks down at the announcement that the man he has all along blamed for his own misfortune is a newly appointed General Authority. As Arthur admits that he is vulnerable because he is unforgiving and that he has all along tried to manipulate his children, they feel freer to recognize their shortcomings and to become reconciled. Arthur's remorse prompts Billy to forget his own bitterness and to console his father. Arthur then asks his sons to bless him, and, as they do so, Mildred and Chris looking on, all are reunited. None of their problems is fully resolved. Billy is still unsure if he will embark on a mission. But the atmosphere is one of peace and mutual compassion, of budding faith. And there is hope.

DRAMATIC MONOLOGUE: 1M(teen) • BILLY -- Act 2
ABOUT THE CHARACTER:
BILLY: This really is the moment of understanding in the play, the point where all can move forward to whatever resolution they may come to. It has taken BILLY a long time to come to this point himself -- for the right reasons.

BILLY: I think you all want me to go on a mission, that's what I think. You all want me to go real bad--but I'm still no longer sure for who or for what reason. You want me to so bad that now you're trying to fool yourselves, not just me, that everything's changed, that the gospel has really made a difference in your lives, that we really are one big happy, caring, self-sacrificing family. But after I've left, what then? Will it really make a lasting difference? Does that precious gospel we're always talking about really make any difference at all? Or is it just a lot of words? Are most of us just hooked on so many words--when the way we actually get along is the pits, a jungle, like everywhere else? At least Chris hasn't totally brainwashed herself. I feel more comfortable with her right now than with any of the rest of you.

DRAMATIC MONOLOGUE: 1M • WAYNE -- Act 1
ABOUT THE CHARACTER:
WAYNE: He is speaking to his brother, Jerold, who seems to have been able to keep it all together, but Wayne sees the cracks that form in every faithful person's life and begins to fault Jerold for that. He is really very envious and unhappy with his own position in life and the Church.

WAYNE: You really worship man instead of God, and that's why everything you do has a practical reason. You keep the Word of Wisdom and go to Sunday School so your children will do the same and won't end up in the drug scene. You claim to love them but you really just don't want them to embarrass or inconvenience you. So you keep them busy in seminary and Young Adults--jumping all the hurdles. You get with them on Monday night for the same reason. Meanwhile they babble about all their silly awards, their good grades, etc., and your wife babbles all day about her domestic superfluities, her fascinating womanhood, because they all desperately want the personal recognition you never really give them. Because you put your career and the things you accumulate before other people. You're really only in love with yourself. Oh, sure, you preach love and harmony and obedience--you're very good at that--but you still default where it really counts: You saddle your wife with the real concern for your kids like any other pharisaical churchman. In the traditional Mormon manner you come across as extremely spiritual. But you're totally self-serving. Even in the Church you try to manipulate everyone else--from Primary kids to high priests. And that's a contradiction I find hard to reconcile.

DRAMATIC SCENE: 1M 1W • CHRIS & WAYNE -- Act 1
ABOUT THE CHARACTER:
CHRIS: the one who was never sure if she had a testimony or

not, the only girl in the family besides Mom (ALICE) she is at a point of inactivity in the Church and not sure what to do about it, if anything. She is engaged to be married, secretly, to a man who is also not a member of the Church and whom the family has never met.

WAYNE: *is very envious of others and unhappy with his own position in life and the Church. He is the one who almost always achieved, but then not quite. He is the grain of sand in the oyster, but when he is spit out he struggles to get back in.*

CHRIS has just received the phone call from her finance. The call was overheard by WAYNE.

CHRIS: Mother didn't sneak in here while I was talking, did she?

WAYNE: Course not.

CHRIS: She didn't eavesdrop?

WAYNE: No. She's not even home. Why? What difference would it make? Your boy friend can call you up if he wants, can't he?

CHRIS: I just don't want the folks to know he's coming. If they do, they'll expect to meet him.

WAYNE: So. ..?

CHRIS: So they might not like him. He smokes. Cigars, in fact.

WAYNE: Come off it, Chris. They're not that prissy--not even Mom.

CHRIS: What about the preacher?

WAYNE: The preacher?

CHRIS: Jerold.

WAYNE: You can handle Jerold--when he comes. He hasn't shown up yet.

CHRIS: That's a relief.

WAYNE: And the others went into town.

CHRIS: What for?

WAYNE: Dad had an appointment with Doc Adams. And Billy needs a suit for his mission.

CHRIS: Dear, sweet Billy. He's the best of the bunch. I hope it won't be too hard on him.

WAYNE: Hard on him?

CHRIS: The way yours was for you...

WAYNE: I'm glad you could be here, Chris. Don't you usually fly on weekends?

CHRIS: That's right. I had to trade shifts with three other girls. But it will be worth it to see Billy up there at that pulpit tomorrow.

WAYNE: I don't believe that.

CHRIS: Why?

WAYNE: The Church doesn't mean that much to you. Not any more.

CHRIS: How do you know?

WAYNE: Actions speak louder, you know.

CHRIS: Well, maybe it doesn't. But Billy does. He means a lot to me. I'd do anything to cheer him on....Is Dad sick again?

WAYNE: Just a routine exam, Mom said.

CHRIS: That's a relief....

(Still pacing)

Even so, damn it!

WAYNE: What?

CHRIS: "Damn it'" I said. "Damn it'" Is that all right?

WAYNE: Sure.

CHRIS: I can do better than that.

WAYNE: Yeah?

CHRIS: What you don't have to listen to just working in the bay or up in the cockpit, or, worst of all, from some fresh passenger who's trying to make out and can't hold his liquor. There's at least one on every flight.

WAYNE: That's what you get for calling them "the friendly skies."

CHRIS: Anyway, I'm in good practice. Wanna hear me?

WAYNE: No.

CHRIS: Okay, I won't defile the dear nest....

WAYNE: What's eating you, Chris? You've gotten pretty hard since you left home.

CHRIS: Look who's talking.

WAYNE: Yeah, I know.

CHRIS: You ever going back to Beverly?

WAYNE: I'm not sure. She'll have to be satisfied with what I earn, which will never be much....If that mother of hers would just keep her nose out of it and quit giving her ideas. Always lambasting me about Bev's wardrobe or getting a more "respectable" car. Or the fact that I'm not a High Priest and didn't complete my mission.

CHRIS: How about Julie?
WAYNE: What about her?
CHRIS: How old is she now?
WAYNE: Almost seven.
CHRIS: She loves you, Wayne. She needs you.
WAYNE: I've been half tempted to quit teaching. Just get lost somewhere and start writing. You know how I've always wanted to.
CHRIS: But you might not make much. Beverly wouldn't accept that.
WAYNE: Would that be so awful....? You ought to understand better than anyone else--free spirit that you are. You should know as well as I how much the Church cramps a person's style and limits his possibilities. It's stifled my whole creative impulse. And it never gave you a fighting chance for the right man in your life.
CHRIS: Am I complaining?
WAYNE: Not in so many words.
CHRIS: Well, then?
WAYNE: I thought we were kindred spirits.
CHRIS: We still are. but I'm not going to chime in and encourage you to turn your back on Julie--or on Beverly for that matter. Maybe I can appreciate what a good thing you've got there more than you can because it's something I've never had--and may never get.
WAYNE: You can have it, Chris--you especially if you want it.
CHRIS: So can you, Wayne....
WAYNE: Well, don't forget--you're the only one who knows we've separated.
CHRIS: I know better than to upset mom or spoil Billy's farewell. Give me that much credit.
WAYNE: Of course you do. And so do I: At all costs, maintain a pleasant facade. In fact, coming here on the plane this time, I made a vow.
CHRIS: A vow?
WAYNE: Not to say one thing out of turn to Jerry. Not even once.
CHRIS: That's good. It can't hurt. It can only help.
WAYNE: Help me keep that vow, will you?
CHRIS: I'll try....Whatcha reading?
WAYNE: *Anna Karenina*.

CHRIS: "Anna" who?

WAYNE: *Karenina.* Tolstoy's finest work--the great European novel.

CHRIS: Oh, yes....It's awful thick. Do you make your students read it?

WAYNE: I wish I could. I'm lucky if I can get them to watch it on TV.

CHRIS: What makes it so special?

WAYNE: The question it poses, I guess.

CHRIS: Question?

WAYNE: About why people behave the way they do--why some make those terribly fateful choices, like Anna's, that lead to their destruction, while others like Levin--

CHRIS: Who?

WAYNE: He's another character in the novel. Why the Levins finally reconcile themselves to God and life.

CHRIS: Like Mormons?

WAYNE: Like *some* Mormons. Listen to this. It's the novel's very first sentence: "All happy families resemble one another, but each unhappy family is unhappy in its own way." How does that grab you?

CHRIS: I don't know. When I look at people that are really unhappy--whole families, I mean--

WAYNE: Like ours?

CHRIS: No. We're basically happy, aren't we?

WAYNE: We pretend to be.

CHRIS: I mean marriages where a man and a woman are so at odds that they haven't spoken to each other or been intimate for months or years--

WAYNE: How would you know about such marriages?

CHRIS: Well, I do. And from what I can tell, the way people like that are unhappy is so much the same from one marriage to the next, so predictable, so unrelieved--it bores me to think about.

WAYNE: I see. The banality of evil.

CHRIS: Something like that. But you tell me, how does Tolstoy answer his own big question? Since you've read the book, and I haven't. Why the man ends up all right, and the woman doesn't?

WAYNE: Tolstoy doesn't tell us. He keeps the whole thing open. That makes it all the more lifelike. Don't you agree? (He returns to his book.)

CHRIS: Wayne?

WAYNE: Huh?

CHRIS: What kept you from being more like Jerold? With the same parents and all?

WAYNE: I can't tell you, Chris. That's another one of those mysteries. Except--remember the Stovers who used to live next door? About the time I became a deacon? You couldn't have been more than seven or eight.

CHRIS: That family from Pennsylvania?

WAYNE: Yes.

CHRIS: They were non-members, weren't they?

WAYNE: Yes. And they had a son named Randy.

CHRIS: Oh, I remember him. He was real cute. I had a crush on him.

WAYNE: He and I were best friends--for a while.

CHRIS: I remember. What happened?

WAYNE: Well, I'd just been made a deacon. And we'd had a lesson about going on a mission. I really got fired up, and I decided that Randy should be a deacon too and I was the one to convert him. His parents were awfully nice to me-- took me along on camping trips and whenever they went anywhere special. To keep him company. We slept over a lot too. Well, one night when I was staying at his house I decided to tell him the Joseph Smith story and bear my testimony.

CHRIS: That's interesting.

WAYNE: What?

CHRIS: You had a testimony then?

WAYNE: Why, yes. I guess I did.

CHRIS: Was it a lie?

WAYNE: A lie?

CHRIS: Were you right then, or are you right now?

WAYNE: We become wiser with age, don't we...?

CHRIS: Well, and then what happened?

WAYNE: Well, I only got half-way through when his mother came into the room. She made some excuse why I ought to go home. Randy wasn't feeling well, or something. I could tell it was a lie.

CHRIS: Your testimony?

WAYNE: No. What she said to me! She was nice enough, but tense. Real tense. So I got out of bed, got dressed, and came

home. They never asked me over again...It's a wonder I ever went on a mission after that. I guess I still didn't know better.
CHRIS: What do you mean?
WAYNE: Nothing...
CHRIS: Wayne?
WAYNE: Yes...?
CHRIS: This Anna--what's her name?
WAYNE: Karenina.
CHRIS: What was her problem?
WAYNE: *(looking at her, hard)* She was an adulteress....
CHRIS: *(staring back, then finally turning away)* Oh...

DRAMATIC SCENE: 2M • BILLY & WAYNE -- Act 1
ABOUT THE CHARACTER:
BILLY: *Has been planning for a mission all his life. But with the tension at home, after the return of his older siblings, he begins to doubt himself, others and the Church.*
WAYNE: *Seems to be the character the author has chosen to bounce everyone's opinion off of, including the audience. He is the likable, yet irritable never satisfied one. Nothing has ever worked for him like it has for the others around him.*

They are at BILLY's home. The same home where WAYNE was raised.
WAYNE: So how's the new elder? Feel any different?
BILLY: Not very. Am I supposed to?
WAYNE: I kind of think you are. Better work on it.
BILLY: I will....Did you? Feel different when they made you an Elder?
WAYNE: No....
BILLY: Oh....Whatcha reading?
WAYNE: A Russian novel. Tolstoy.
BILLY: I wanted to go there on my mission.
WAYNE: Russia?
BILLY: Yeah. But we still don't have a mission there.
WAYNE: Well, you should enjoy Mexico. You'll probably have

lots of baptisms.
BILLY: You think so?
WAYNE: Yes....
   (He returns to his book.)
BILLY: Wayne?
WAYNE: Uh huh...?
BILLY: What was your mission like? I've never heard you talk about it.
WAYNE: It was all right....
BILLY: Just "all right"?
WAYNE: It was okay.
BILLY: What does that mean?
WAYNE: Some days were all right. Some were a waste.
BILLY: Was that because you didn't always have the Spirit with you?
WAYNE: Maybe. I don't know.
BILLY: I won't let that happen.
WAYNE: I hope you won't, Billy. In fact, I hope that when you come home you can say that your mission was the single most inspiring time of your entire life.
BILLY: Can't you say that--about your mission?
WAYNE: Not if I don't want to lie to you....
   (Billy tries to say something but is too perplexed.)
But some people can. Ask Jerold when he comes. That's exactly how he'll put it. Some RM's say "the best" or "the most wonderful" but Jerry--Jerold always says,"It was the single most inspiring time of my entire life." Not just "the most inspiring time." But "the *single* most inspiring time of my entire life!
BILLY: Will he use those exact same words?
WAYNE: Wait and see....Still want to be a doctor some day, Billy?
BILLY: I sure do.
WAYNE: Why?
BILLY: Well, we'll always need doctors, won't we?
WAYNE: I suppose we will.
BILLY: You can do a lot of good for people.
WAYNE: Especially for yourself. It's a pretty good life--I'm sure you've noticed.
BILLY: Doctors work long hours, Wayne. They're always on

call. And look at Doc Adams -- he helps a lot of people out and never sends them a bill. Dad for one.

WAYNE: And wins everyone's respect and devotion--without ever really straining himself. He can still afford his Cadillac, his weekends in Palm Springs, his membership in the country club. And it's all good P.R. -- like a charitable tax write-off.

BILLY: I don't follow you, Wayne. Doc Adams earns everything he gets.

WAYNE: Maybe so, Billy. But there's a vast difference between those who do good 'to be seen of men' and those rare souls--wherever you find them--they're this world's true Saints--who totally invest themselves in others' lives. Take Albert Schweitzer, for example. Or that woman from Albania.

BILLY: Albania?

WAYNE: That Catholic nun who somehow had the vision thirty or so years ago to leave the slums of Skopje and go where life was even worse.

BILLY: Where was that?

WAYNE: India. But not just anywhere in India. To its very cesspool. The 'black hole'.

BILLY: Where's that?

WAYNE: Calcutta. To give dying people a little comfort and a shred of dignity as they leave this life....

BILLY: I remember now. She was in the papers a while back, wasn't she?

WAYNE: She got the Nobel Peace Prize. But you can bet she didn't expect to when she went to India.

BILLY: So what's the point?

WAYNE: The point? Well, you're one of God's elect, aren't you? One of his chosen servants?

BILLY: I...I guess.

WAYNE: You guess?

BILLY: I mean, sure I am.

WAYNE: Then you should be as saintly as that nun, shouldn't you? She doesn't even call herself a Saint, but you do....

BILLY: I'll be glad to go on a health mission for the Church some day--after I become a doctor.

WAYNE: That so?

BILLY: Sure....

WAYNE: *(disappointed)* I see.

A Sceptre, A Sword, A Scented Rose
A Play by *Thom Duncan*

ABOUT THE PLAY: The story of Ammon and King Lamoni as recounted in ALMA 17-19. Ammon, a Nephite son of King Mosiah, ventures into the Land Of Ishmael on missionary endeavors. He's captured and brought before the wicked Lamanite vassal King, Lamoni, who is enthralled by this Nephite's courage and strength. Lamoni keeps Ammon as one of his servants, soon promoting him to his private man. Lamoni's conversion to the True Gospel is the climax to this suspenseful play.

<u>*DRAMATIC MONOLOGUE: 1W • ABISH -- Act 1*</u>
ABOUT THE CHARACTER:
ABISH: she is the servant to the Queen, SEPHARIAH. She is a Believer, but mostly has to hide that fact as Believers are put to death in this society. Here she talks to Ammon. She has told him about her Faith; taken a chance that he will not betray her. This is her conversion story.

ABISH: It was to protect Father. I swore him to silence in fear they might slay him. He sent me here, for when I told him you were from Zarahemla, he would not be quieted until I promised I would bring you to him. The fire was kindled long before you came, before Lamoni came to power. Two Nephites came to us, preaching and expounding this great Nephite god who could speak and see and resembled a man. The first time I saw them, it was one day while Father and I were going to market; I had a hold of his hand as we passed the steps of the Temple of Nehor. There was a small crowd gathered about the streets of the city, so I pulled on his hand and we stopped and listened. Some of the crowd began to surge up in anger against them. Soon, all were jeering and laughing -- some pushed and shoved -- one of the Nephites was knocked down, I remember. My mother had died some years before. Father called her his "Dear Tellah." She put up with him so much, his moods, she waited on him at all hours of the day or night. He strongly felt her absence in our household. Wherefore, as we heard the words of the Nephites, his heart took again new hope. What they said was so clear and not draped with sacred mysteries. They came secretly and placed before us the truth we have so long time embraced. For Father, it was the fact that he would see again his "dear Tellah." That night my father was caught up in a vision, wherein he saw Mother calling him, beckoning him. "How may I be where you are?" he asked. "Where I am, you cannot come, save you should hearken unto the Nephites and be baptized." I've wanted so long to tell it to someone. Penned up inside for such a long time, I could not control it.

MONOLOGUE: 1M • LAMONI -- Act 2
ABOUT THE CHARACTER:

LAMONI: A man caught between the greatest truth he could ever hope to understand and the lies and traditions of his forefathers. But his heart is still able, through much tribulation, to see truth and be humbly taught.

LAMONI: Has my vision come to a close? Am I no more to be plagued by Ammon's god?
    (A pause)
What? No answer? Each time before, little time was wasted in assailing me with unpleasant memories. Whence comes this present dearth of torture? Hast thou, the infinite "God" used up thy power? Or art thou only temporarily staying thy hand, to unleash anew when thy whim demands it?
    (A pause)
I fear it not, O Ammon's God! Send forth thy onslaught. Thinkest thou to break me with demons real or imagined? I, the mightiest warrior among all the Lamanites?
    (Another pause. Lamoni's demeanor greatly softens)

She loveth me. I knew it not before. Or, knowing, I did not acknowledge it. How at peace this knowing puts me. Sephariah a proud and haughty woman, she. Naught but greater love than self could bring her to her knees before Ammon. Is there a sign there, to show me the way of deliverance? On her knees before the Nephite. Myself on my knees before his God? Is this the purpose of his God, the way?

> *(He kneels, slowly; it is the hardest thing in the world for him to do. Suddenly, he arises, moving away.)*

Nay, a Lamanite King does not kneel before a Nephite God. I care not that I should sleep for eternity, I shall not heap humiliation upon myself!

> *(Pause)*

Sephariah! Do not waste such pleading on such as I! Great warrior I may be, but also puppet King and figurehead husband. Thy tears deserve greater men to fall upon! Thy love for me is a mystery, when all thine affections have been turned back upon thee in spite and hate. Wherefore lovest thou me still? Is the fountain of a woman's love endless? Is it that it flows continually, mindful not of whom it falls upon, or how its cooling spray is received? Could this be so? A sign in that, as well, it seemeth me. Like Sephariah and her love for me, the same is Ammon's God? Can it be that he loveth me still? A strange love, this, when he chastiseth his children. I want no such love. Love me not, God! I will refuse it.

> *(A pause)*

What is this, that fills my bosom? This warmth that surgeth within my frame?

> *(He grabs his chest, lurches his feet.)*

It is thou, Ammon's God. Thou smitest me for my refusal.

> *(He cries out and falls to his knees.)*

Nay, this feeling is like unto what overcame me when Ammon called my name. God, thou has brought me to my knees after all; it was not force, but the same persuasion that Ammon used to bring me to this state. It is nigh too much to bear, this purity which invades my unworthy temple.

> *(A pause)*

O, God, that I might be made to withstand thy presence, for that is surely what encompasseth me. Strip me of my sinful garb, and place me on the path to peace within. Raise me up that I might make amends unto Sephariah, that we may rebuild the lives we almost lost! Cause that I may have the great power of Ammon, which power is greater than all my armies! O God, Ammon's God -- my God, release my chains of bondage!

DRAMATIC SCENE: 2W • SEPHARIAH & ABISH -- Act 1
ABOUT THE CHARACTER:
SEPHARIAH: The Queen of the Lamanites and Lamoni's wife. She is concerned with outward appearance and how she is perceived. This is, in part, due to her position, but her position has caused a great pride to well up in her. Yes, she can be tender to those whom she loves.

ABISH: she is the servant to the Queen, SEPHARIAH. She is a Believer, but mostly has to hide that fact as Believers are put to death in this society. Always fearful at being discovered, she lives her life among the ungodly, hoping and praying for the day of deliverance.

SEPHARIAH: Abish! Abish!
   (ABISH ENTERS carrying some gowns.)
ABISH: Yes, my lady?
SEPHARIAH: This gown is sticking me! Fix it!
ABISH: I see no pin.
SEPHARIAH: It's sticking me, I tell you! Find it!
ABISH: Now I see it. But the Queen must not move.
SEPHARIAH: Pull it out!
ABISH: There! I have it!
SEPHARIAH: I have spoken with the King. Your mare is being prepared.
ABISH: Very well.
SEPHARIAH: Which gowns are we taking?
ABISH: I had thought perhaps these.
SEPHARIAH: They will do... but you have failed to pack my favorite, the violet satin with roses.

ABISH: I am repairing it. It will be ready in time for the journey. Shall I pack them?

SEPHARIAH: Of course, you shall pack them! How do you suppose I carry them otherwise?

(Abish bows, starts to EXIT.)

ABISH: As you wish, my Queen.

SEPHARIAH: Abish, dear Abish. You will not allow me to be angry with you. The more I lash out, the gentler you become and my anger ebbs.

ABISH: I wish only to keep my Queen happy.

SEPHARIAH: I would that you teach your ways to the King, for he has not made me happy this long while. Do you know what he has done now? He has taken a Nephite as his servant.

ABISH: A Nephite, my lady?

SEPHARIAH: From Zarahemla My name will be had for mockery in all the land for allowing him to do it! Even now, I can hear the words of belittlement that will come against me at the feast: "Sephariah, are you losing you hand over Lamoni? He no longer comes panting to your side when you roll your eyes?" I will not give those jealous wives the satisfaction of gloating in my failures!

ABISH: The King must have a worthy motive, for doing this thing.

SEPHARIAH: It is well that you are so convinced of my husband's honorable doings!

ABISH: I meant no implication that you do not understand him.

SEPHARIAH: Meant or no, it's true; Lamoni has become a stranger to me.

ABISH: Does not a King have many things to ponder in his mind?

SEPHARIAH: Indeed! But have you noticed the many times he sits, either talking to himself or saying nothing? These seven days past, he has worsened. And then, of a sudden, when he flares up, lamenting and moaning, and bewailing his fate, making such hideous sounds I cannot bear to listen! When he is himself again I confront him with what I have seen and he denies it, saying I have invented it to spite him...! Oh, Abish, how I long for days gone by, when Lamoni and his Queen were first wed, when their love was barely blooming... Now, the blossom has withered, the petals have fallen to dust, and the whole of it is blown away by the winds of discontent... Could I but recapture that early bliss, somehow remove the years. But no monarch, regardless of the vastness of his empire, has the power to alter what time has wrought.

ABISH: Time is verily the King of us all, my Queen.

SEPHARIAH: I have withstood his ramblings, his upheavals, his casting aside of my efforts to help him, his -- amusements -- but this I will not endure! There must be a way whereby I may undo his consent to this man, Ammon, bring disfavor to him that Lamoni will see his error.-- Go! Pack away the gowns! Make ready!

DRAMATIC SCENE: 1M 1W • AMMON & ABISH -- Act 1
ABOUT THE CHARACTERS:
AMMON: The great missionary of the Book of Mormon. He is young and vital and it is easy for many to believe on his words because he has the gift, something he acquired; it was not born in him, or if it was he ignored it for a long time, until through his own personal anguish, he came to know the truth -- the truth he spreads now for his God.
ABISH: she is the servant to the Queen, SEPHARIAH. She is a Believer, but mostly has to hide that fact as Believers are put to death in this society. But around AMMON she does not have to maintain the pretense. They have become good friends.

(LIGHTS up on Abish's quarters. The room is empty. A beat. Abish ENTERS quietly, looking about. She sees Moriami's vacant chair, then goes to his bedroom, off. Returning, she waves Ammon on. Ammon ENTERS.)

ABISH: He sleeps. If you were to come back another time.

AMMON: I will stay awhile! So seldom do we get the chance to talk. This week past, since that day in the forest, it's been as though you had wings, fluttering about, everywhere except where I am.

ABISH: The final preparations for the journey to Olgatha.

Well, you cannot stay long. If you were discovered--
AMMON: Nothing! Lamoni allows me all freedom and cares not with whom I share it.
ABISH: Lamoni, yes. But Sephariah is not so easily satisfied?
AMMON: Because I did not fall in love with her daughter?
ABISH: *(After an awkward pause)* Isn't it always the way with these things? Plans are made, wardrobes packed, horses prepared, but nothing is done till the last.
AMMON: Much time is wasted making excuses to approach it until oftentimes it is too late.
ABISH: *(Ignoring his flirtations)* A year ago, this time, the halls of the palace were filled with servants running to and fro, gowns swishing the air on their way to the caravan, horses tugging at their reigns in the stables. Every year it is the same.
AMMON: Not every year. Last year, I was in Zarahemla, we had not met and I was the unhappiest of men because of it.
ABISH: Are all Nephites as subtle as you?
AMMON: Ah, subtlety. One quality I lack.
ABISH: Only one? I find humility another which is vacant in you.
AMMON: My arrogance offends you? Alas, such has always been the case in my dealings with women; they mistake a sureness of my abilities for conceit.
ABISH: One who is sure of his abilities does not have to announce it.
AMMON: Nor have I patience.
ABISH: If we go much longer at this, perhaps you will climb down to the level of the rest of us.
AMMON: Then would you pay attention to me?
ABISH: My interest in you is for what you can do for my father. Beyond that, I find no common desires.
AMMON: How long have you been taking care of your father?
ABISH: I count not the years.
AMMON: What have you done for yourself?
ABISH: How do you mean?
AMMON: During these many years you have been nurse, mother, and maid to your father, have you once thought of yourself, what you wanted in life?
ABISH: My life is my father.
AMMON: Your life is your own!

ABISH: I cannot believe these words come from a disciple of our Lord. Is it not taught that we are to love one another, to serve our --

AMMON: I am sorry. I spoke too swift that which was on my mind. Tact is not in me, either.

ABISH: Thereby making three virtues you lack!

AMMON: Of course, your father needs care, but not at the expense of yourself. A man, or woman, too concerned on one thing, no matter how righteous, does detriment to his soul.

ABISH: Wherefore, I should share my concern with you?

AMMON: You said the very words that were on my tongue. Divide your time with me and your fear of men will soon leave!

ABISH: I do not fear men!

AMMON: Know you why you are so devoted to your father? True, part of your desires is to his welfare; I knew you from the first to be a woman with much love in her heart for others less fortunate than she.

(Ammon moves closer to her. Abish moves away.)

But also you have tried to bury yourself in your service, hoping that no man will realize your beauty and charm. You cannot hide it from me. Though I lack many qualities, to know beauty is a virtue with which I *am* blessed.

ABISH: To know the thoughts of others, as well, it would appear.

AMMON: In Zarahemla, we wear not our feelings on the inside, but express them openly, with no fear of being misunderstood.

ABISH: How great must be your love for self, that you assume I would find you to my liking!

AMMON: I cannot forget the delicate timing of your interruption in the forest. Why did you wait so long before breaking in at the moment of our passion if not that you were loathe to see me kissing Zephonia?

ABISH: In truth, I did take pity upon Zephonia, that she was throwing herself upon such a bloated ego as your own!

AMMON: I am not alone in ability to read the thoughts of others, it would seem.

ABISH: Your actions are what I see, the way you carry yourself, your manner of speech, that almost unnoticeable smirk in your smile. These all speak to me of your vanity.

AMMON: If I am so intolerable, why have you scrutinized my actions with such persistence? I regret if I am the cause of ill-feelings; my coming here was to be one of joy , and I have brought only pain. Let's speak no more upon the matter.
 (He notices Abish's flower box, in which roses bloom.)
 Ah! Zephonia has shared with you her love for growing things.
ABISH: They are my own. I am able to share my attention on things other than Father.
AMMON: I have never seen roses so red and luxurious.
ABISH: When despair overcomes me, I come and work with my roses, plowing up the soil with my fingers, and soon I am happy again.
AMMON: But roses live not forever.
ABISH: They remind me of the gentle love that was preached unto me so long ago. The sceptre of the King, meaning great power, the sword in your sheath, much strength and killing... but in a scented rose there is meekness, and a vision of life.
 (Ammon, touching the roses, nicks his finger on a thorn, making an appropriate sound.)
 See what you've done!
 (She takes his hand in hers.)
 You've sliced your finger!
AMMON: Your vision of life is not without its hurtful side.
ABISH: Here, squeeze your finger!
 (She squeezes his finger, holding it over the flower bed, then she takes some soil and rubs that on his finger.)
 That should soothe it.
AMMON: It does. The pain is miraculously gone.
 (Abish tries to pull away her hand, but Ammon has it tight in his own.)
ABISH: You did that expressly!
AMMON: *(Laughs)* You're delightful! One moment you are angry, the next, when you suppose I have hurt myself, you are kind!
ABISH: Any pain I will soothe -- a dog with inflicted paw.
AMMON: Then soothe my pain.
 (Abish looks at his hand.)
 Not there.

ABISH: *(Backs away)* I must see if Father is well.
AMMON: I do please you, do I not?
ABISH: I heard him groan!
AMMON: Abish!
ABISH: My roses!
AMMON: Think of yourself, your own desires, just once!
> *(He kisses her. At first she struggles, then she gives in and their kiss is long and deep. After awhile, they pull apart. Abish slowly sits, then stands and goes over to the roses, plowing the soil, Ammon is watching her all this time. She straightens her hair, then turns, stands looking at Ammon. A beat; she runs into his arms.)*

ABISH: I want to stay here.
AMMON: But your roses.
ABISH: The petals can fall off and the soil dry up. I will stay here, within your arms.

DRAMATIC SCENE: 2M • AMMON & LAMONI -- Act 2
ABOUT THE CHARACTER:
AMMON: The great missionary of the Book of Mormon. His youthful and vital testimony is hard to ignore. His physical presence is stunning. But it is his humble spirit that wins people over.
LAMONI: The great Lamanite King who has murdered and plotted but found something interesting in this enemy Nephite -- almost as a cat with a canary -- he toys with AMMON, until the moment of his conversion.

LAMONI: *(A long pause)* Now you know my burden.
AMMON: What would you that I should do, O King?
> *(Lamoni is silent. The weight of the world seems upon his shoulders.)*

Is it because you have heard how I defended your flocks and servants?
> *(Lamoni looks up, awestruck.)*

What is it, that your marvelings are so great? Behold, I am a man and am your servant. Whatsoever you desire which is right, that will I do.

LAMONI: How is that you discern my thoughts?
> *(A pause)*

Who are you? Are you that Great Spirit, who knows all things?

AMMON: I am not.

LAMONI: Are you indeed the son of King Mosiah?
> *(Silence)*

Leave me! Away from my sight!

AMMON: What have I done to offend my King?

LAMONI: That which I have commanded you, far surpassing my expectations. I would enjoy having you slain but I cannot kill a prince. Wherefore I banish you from the kingdom!

AMMON: Banished?

LAMONI: Go back to Mosiah, your rightful father, O thief of mine affection! I want no more of you here! My life has been but one upheaval followed by another since you came. Antihamnah spoke the truth: you have bewitched me and yet I know not how. Indeed this infirmity, this affliction of my soul and body, came with you!

> *(Lamoni moves to strike him, but recovers. Ammon doesn't even flinch.)*

AMMON: Your life was happy before I came?

LAMONI: It is worse now! When you talk to me, I am confused with your words! Simple words, sharp commands these I understand. But your gentle words turn me away from purposes!

AMMON: Lamoni, it is useless to fight against the bonds.

LAMONI: What do you mean?

AMMON: It is done.

LAMONI: Then speak boldly concerning such a gentle power, wherein a King is cut down by serving him. Tell me by what power you smote the arms of robbers. Be it magic, some occult power you have learned? Set me at ease concerning this, and whatsoever you desire I will grant it.

AMMON: Will you hearken unto my words? That is the thing I desire of you.

LAMONI: Such was your desire from the beginning, was it not? Had I been wise, I would have slain you before the words, before that imputable persuasion of yours compelled me to listen.

(Almost in pain)
A spell, Ammon! You have woven about me a spell that I cannot rend! I shall surely die if you do not enlighten me! Yea, anything! I will believe your words!

AMMON: Do you believe there is a God?

LAMONI: God? Do you mean the Nephite god?

AMMON: The Great Spirit, this is God, the same who created all things which are in heaven and in the earth.

LAMONI: Yea! Yea! I believe it! But I know not the heavens.

AMMON: The place where God dwells, and he looks down upon all the children of men, and he knows all the thoughts and intents of the heart.

LAMONI: This God he sent you?

AMMON: I am a man, created after the image of God, and I am called by the Holy Spirit to teach these things unto this people. And a portion of that spirit dwells in me, and also power. By this did I accomplish these things of which you marvel.

LAMONI: Your disdain for things sacred broaches blasphemy, to suppose the Great Spirit would share with you his power.

AMMON: It is this power that did begin to work upon you before I! came, causing your deeds to well before you, your remorse.

LAMONI: Remorse, is it? I am no stranger to that! I would pride myself on the manner in which I once laughed at death, but now wherefore was I plagued by attackers in my sleep?

AMMON: Past deeds brought to remembrance that you might be humbled.

LAMONI: This God of yours, does he always work in ways so devious, against a human will?

(Lamoni turns away.)

AMMON: Lamoni.

LAMONI: You speak my name, and peace floods my every being. Ammon, that I may have this strength in meekness, for such pain I cannot long endure. There must be a purpose to your god, a way? Show it to me, Ammon! Give this king a reason for rescue!

AMMON: You have the reason, deep within yourself. Search within. You shall find it.

LAMONI: Your god, does he delight in the despair of his creatures? Has he sent you here to torment me? What shall

I give you to tell me the path to peace? My Kingdom? You may have it! With all its perplexities, it is far less than the mantle I am called to wear! My jewels? They are yours! Take them, take them all, only RELIEVE ME! You blind a king who has befriended you then will not give him back his sight? I could take my sceptre and break it over your back!

DRAMATIC SCENE: 2M • JAKOR & LAMONI -- Act 1 Scene One
ABOUT THE CHARACTER:
JAKOR: is the physician to LAMONI's court. He is often obsequious and willing to please -- he has to be to keep his head.
LAMONI: The great Lamanite King who is a ruthless ruler until AMMON comes into his life and unsettles him.

LAMONI: What is it, Jakor?
JAKOR: The Queen Sephariah came to me this morning in a somewhat agitated state of mind and remained that way for several moments. When I was finally able to calm her sufficiently, she began to lay before me the resume of your seemingly inexplicable actions of late, whereupon I promptly came to you to conclude for myself and discover that her most feared intuitions are true. The King is indeed ill.
LAMONI: And what is his ailment, physician?
JAKOR: Were the King to answer my questions, I could --
LAMONI: Very well, ask your questions.
JAKOR: How long have you been suffering from such spells?
LAMONI: Spells? Spells? What spells?
JAKOR: These... er... moments when your awareness takes wings -- figuratively speaking, of course -- and flies from you like a bird from its nest.
LAMONI: That is impossible to answer since, my awareness having taken wings figuratively speaking, of course -- and flying from me like a bird, etcetera -- I am unaware that

they occur.

JAKOR: Seven days, the Queen says.

LAMONI: Then I have suffered from these spells since seven days!

JAKOR: Perhaps the King is not concerned over his condition, but, as physician to the court, I must needs inquire.

LAMONI: Then go and inquire of the Queen, who seems to know more about my condition than either one of us!

JAKOR: *(Dauntless, ever dauntless)* Has the King noticed a failing of his strength -- any matter of vertigo?

LAMONI: Jakor, I fear the Queen, however pure her motives may appear, has misinformed you.

JAKOR: Would that I be the judge of that. After all, it is my responsibility, my necessary function.

LAMONI: I've got it! Sephariah has conspired with you to prove me a fool! Oh, what a bothersome woman, living from one day to the next to make my life insufferable!

JAKOR: I sensed grave concern in her tones.

LAMONI: One of her favorite tricks. In one breath, she is the perfect picture of sincerity, an image imposed for us that she might gain her own ends! She has not a heart within her bosom, but a stone.

JAKOR: Have there been times when --

LAMONI: Jakor, I see not the point behind this interrogation.

JAKOR: *(Hurt)* Unfortunate. Truly unfortunate. I seek only your improved health.

LAMONI: *(Tired)* And for what reason? That you may prescribe what you always prescribe -- a lifeless metal charm placed around the neck, a seasoning of senseless terms sprinkled about my ears? Look at me, Jakor! Is this the body of an ill man? Notice with what ease I move about! There are many close to me in years and even younger whose shriveled legs can barely keep them from faltering! Still power in these bones! And do not forget that the King you see before you goes into battle with his army behind him. I am much known for my fierceness in combat; the land is laden yet with the bodies of those I have felled with my own sword! Are these the doings of a man in need of a physician? Jakor, I think you would better use your time to consult the books and relearn your art.

Stones
A Play by *J. Scott Bronson*

ABOUT THE PLAY: Two hour long plays make up thing intensely moving and spiritual piece. The second play, Tombs, presents Jesus and his Mother, Mary, along with Joseph in a riveting manner. You see the Eternal nature of the Savior amid his earthly humanness. The first play, is the story of Abraham, Isaac and Sarai -- the very Type of Christ and the Sacrifice that was to be made. These stories are talked of side by side in all discussions about the Atonement. Now, here they are 'side-by-side' in a play.

<u>DRAMATIC SCENE: 2M • FATHER (ABRAHAM), SON (ISAAC)</u>
ABOUT THE CHARACTERS:
ABRAHAM: the patriarch, fears most that his son will have to go through just what he did so many years ago.
ISAAC: eager and trusting, which is why he was chosen.

FROM "ALTARS" (The First Act of the play STONES.)

SON: Has God told you if you will have another son?
  (Pause.)
FATHER: No.
SON: No, you're not, or no, He hasn't?
FATHER: He has said nothing about it.
SON: Then we're proceeding blindly?
FATHER: What do you mean?
SON: How will you father a nation without a son? Or will it be through my brother after all?
FATHER: I don't know. I had thought -- I had hoped -- I've always believed that it would be through you.
SON: Isn't that what he promised?
FATHER: I've always assumed that. Perhaps I was wrong.
SON: But you've kept your part of the covenant. You removed the foreskin of every male of your household, including yourself, and me when I was eight days old. You have

fulfilled your part. How will he fulfill his?

FATHER: He satisfied one impossible demand by giving me you. He can satisfy another.

SON: Mother was already long past birthing age when I was born and it's been more than thirty years since then. How can her body accommodate?

FATHER: You know the answer to that.

SON: Yes. The Lord will provide.
> *(Pause.)*

Oh, Father, please don't make me do this.

FATHER: I won't. But it must be done.
> *(Pause.)*

SON: I know.
> *(Pause.)*

I have known from the moment you announced that we were taking a journey how this journey would end.

FATHER: How could you have known? I gave nothing away. Even your mother did not suspect, and she knows me better than I know myself. If she had known we never would have gotten away. How did you know?

SON: I begged the issue. I boasted.
> *(Pause.)*

I was swollen with pride and the Lord took me at my word.

FATHER: What are you talking about?

SON: My brother was speaking highly of himself --

FATHER: Your brother often speaks highly of himself.

SON: Well, occasionally it gets to be too much for me.

FATHER: Me too.

SON: Then you can understand what a temptation it is to challenge his pride.

FATHER: Yes. I can understand.
> *(Pause.)*

What was he puffed up about this time?

SON: His circumcision.
> *(Pause.)*

FATHER: Is it better than yours?

SON: If you ask him, yes.

FATHER: How is that?

SON: I was but eight days old, a mere infant when my foreskin was removed. I don't remember the pain.

FATHER: Ah. And I assume he told you that he bore the pain as a man, not like a bawling child?

SON: Of course.
FATHER: Of course. The truth is that he wasn't quite that aged and, although he was a sturdy boy, on this occasion he wasn't exactly the man he pretended to be. I would not say that is necessarily shameful, however, for circumcision is indeed a painful process to endure and I believe I may have shed a tear or two myself over the matter.
SON: I wish I had known that before I boasted of my own capacity to bear pain.
(Pause.)
I said to him that if God should require it, I would willingly lay down my life, as a sacrifice, upon a burning altar.
(Pause.)
God must have been listening.
FATHER: Or your brother told him.
SON: He doesn't often speak to the Lord as far as I know. Though he may have in this case.
(Pause. Falling to his knees:)
Father, help me.
(The FATHER goes to the SON. The SON embraces the FATHER about the knees. The FATHER holds the SON's head in his hands.)
FATHER: I know, child. I'm sorry.
(Pause.)
I love you. You will --
(Pause.)
The Lord will --
(Pause.)
I --
(Pause.)
I can't --
(Pause.)
I can't -- I can't believe the Lord wants me to do this. I mean --
(Pause.)
SON: Why, Father?
FATHER: Why? Why would a true god require that a man kill his own son? That is only in the purview of invented gods of stone and clay.
SON: But the true god has required it, hasn't he?
FATHER: Yes. But I don't know why. It makes no sense. It's

wrong.

SON: Can the true god command us to do something that is wrong?

FATHER: I -- I suspect I don't know the answer to that any more. But it is the question that has haunted me -- tortured me -- for three days. Since the moment we left your mother standing there, in front of her tent, smiling ... confident of your return.

(Pause.)

Your mother believes she will see you again.

SON: She will.

FATHER: In this life!

(Pause.)

If I can not take you back to her, as you are now, alive -- full of warm blood and ... passions -- how can I return to her at all? How?

(Pause.)

SON: But how can we disobey God?

FATHER: Like that! In an instant. We can pick up the wood, we can pick up the fire, and we can walk back down the side of this mountain, and I can take you to your mother's tent and ... and ...

SON: God won't allow that.

FATHER: Oh yes, He will. He will allow us to do anything we choose to do. He allowed one man to kill his brother in cold blood simply because of jealousy. Because, you see, the flesh and the blood of man is not as important as the spirit of man --

SON: Which is why we must do this.

FATHER: True. You're ... true.

(Pause.)

SON: Father, I don't want to die.

(Pause.)

But I will.

FATHER: Oh, dying's easy. You don't need strength to die. You need strength to live. You need even more strength to kill ... your own son.

(Pause.)

SON: If the Lord has required it then will he not strengthen you for it?

FATHER: Yes. Of course. If I ask him.

SON: Then do it.

FATHER: I don't want to.

<u>*DRAMATIC SCENE: 1M 1W • SON (JESUS), MOTHER (MARY)*</u>
ABOUT THE CHARACTERS:
JESUS: The perfect Son, God's Son, knowing and sometimes apprehensive about what He knows is going to happen and just how He is supposed to accomplish it all.
MARY: knows of her Son's destiny, his Mission, has known since before His birth, has done her best to prepare Him for it, but did she take the time to prepare herself?

From "Tombs" (The Second Act of the play "STONES")

MOTHER: I have never been so frightened. Not before or since ... until now. What's going to happen?
SON: Mother, you have no need to fear. I am in Father's hands.
MOTHER: You've said that before ... and I believe it. But, for some reason, it doesn't comfort me.
SON: Comfort will come. In its own time.
MOTHER: Everything in its season. Is that it?
SON: Yes.
MOTHER: Is your season upon us?
SON: Yes.
MOTHER: What does that mean?
SON: It means I will be leaving soon.
MOTHER: To do what?
SON: Teach. As you said, I'm a teacher.
MOTHER: Where will you go?
SON: Everywhere Father leads me.
MOTHER: Will I ever see you again?
SON: Oh yes. You will see me.
MOTHER: When will you leave?
SON: Soon.
    (Pause.)
MOTHER: Please don't.
SON: Mother --

MOTHER: I don't want you to go --
SON: This is what I was born to do.
    (Pause.)
MOTHER: I know.
SON: Do you?
MOTHER: Yes.
SON: You know the purpose of my existence?
MOTHER: Of course.
SON: How do you know?
MOTHER: You're not the only one to receive visitors.
SON: HI know that, but ... I thought -- I was told…
MOTHER: What?
SON: That I was the only one who knew about ...
MOTHER: That you're the Mediator? That you will be despised and persecuted of men? That you will bear the burden of the world and men will want to kill you? Yes, I know about that. I've heard you and others read the scriptures. I know what they mean. I know who you are. And what you are. At least I think I do. Maybe there's more to it.
    (Pause.)
I love you. You can't know how much I love you. You can't know how badly I need you right now. You can't leave.
    (Pause.)
You say nothing.
SON: I don't want to hurt you, Mother.
MOTHER: Oh, you could never hurt me. There was a great deal of pain when you were born ... but never has there been an ounce of hurt.
    (Pause.)
It's strange to think about, but I imagine some day people will celebrate your birth. There will be songs written about the beauty of that holy night. About the angels who sang. About the shepherds and the inn -- the kings from the east. But no one will sing about the blood and the pain and the sweat and the pain and the tears and that incredible pain. But it was all a part of it. They'll sing about the manger and the gently lowing cattle, but they won't sing about the hearty scent of animal dung. About the grunting and the groaning. They will see your birth as a miracle and they will assume that it was silent and easy. They won't ever imagine that you came into this world just like every other

babe that is born, through the bloody, watery womb of a screeching, straining mortal woman of flesh and bone. The miracle of your birth is who your father is, not your mother.

SON: No, Mother. No man could have done what you did. Not even the Eternal Man who is my father. If he could have he would have.

(Pause.)

Only a woman. And he chose you. Do you know what it means in all Father's creations He chose you to bear the son of God? That He trusted you to raise him to be a god?

(Pause.)

You are the greatest miracle of my life. Believe that.

MOTHER: I'll try.

(Pause.)

I wish your brothers and sisters felt the same way.

SON: *(Laughing.)* Some day they will. Give them time.

MOTHER: Oh yes, on my death bed they'll all be gathered around uttering whispered prayers assuring God and me that they honor me as the greatest miracle of their lives.

SON: Yes, I believe they will. And they'll mean it. Just as I do, with all my heart, mind and soul.

MOTHER: Thank you.

(Pause. She kisses him. Touches his face, his hair.)

You are a miracle too.

SON: Yes, well, a child born of a virgin is a rather miraculous thing.

MOTHER: That's not what I mean. To me you were the most ... I don't know. It's impossible to describe. Just to touch your perfect, smooth skin. To look into your eyes and try to imagine what you were thinking. To watch you crawl around picking up everything in your path and putting it in your mouth. Everything about you was, still is, a miracle to me.

SON: Even if I were not the Son of God you would feel that way. A mother's first child ... well, if you can't describe it, how can I?

MOTHER: Perhaps you're right. Perhaps the miracle is in discovering how to be a mother.

SON: Then every mother everywhere could know that miracle if they would follow your example.

MOTHER: I don't deserve that.

SON: Of course you --
(She stops him with a gesture.)
MOTHER: Please don't. I appreciate and cherish your honor for me. It is a wonderful gift, especially coming from you. But, any more than that is ... too much. I'm afraid I wouldn't believe even you if you were to bestow me with more praise than I deserve. I could never live up to it. I may allow you to call me a miracle or even an angel ... maybe. But never ... never the perfect mother.
SON: But to me --
MOTHER: Don't!
(Pause.)
Listen, if you're going to begin teaching people, there's something you need to understand about people. We don't love better by reaching for perfection. We approach perfection by loving better. Does that make sense?
SON: Perfect sense.
MOTHER: Was that meant to be funny?
SON: Possibly.
MOTHER: Now that I think about it, I suppose it is possible that to you I might have seemed like a perfect mother because I did love you so very much. But it was easy to love you. So easy.
SON: More than the others?
MOTHER: It must seem that way. But not really. It's just that ... my heart went out to you so much. I was always so afraid for you.
SON: Why?
MOTHER: Because ... because ... you're so submissive. To a parent, that's ... a dream come true, a completely obedient child. Who couldn't be grateful for that? But you tended to let people take advantage of you. I hated that. You always seemed to be in so much pain. And I can't bear to see you in pain.
SON: And yet, every pain that I brought to you over the years -- every cut, scrape, bruise and hurt feeling that I had was soothed, treated, kissed and healed by your love.

A Teenage Witness To The Martyrdom
A Short Musical by *C. Michael Perry*

ABOUT THE PLAY: Jason Chamberlin is a 14 year old boy who is struggling to forget the recent death of his father by mob action against the Saints of Missouri. He and his Mother, sisters and brother now live in Nauvoo where the hatred of the Mormons is again beginning to rear it's ugly head. He is also struggling with his testimony and his basic belief in God. Through the help of his family and Joseph Smith he sees that he isn't the only one who is suffering. He has always worshipped Joseph almost like he worshipped his father. His father and Joseph were friends. Soon, he finds himself present as the mob massacres Joseph and Hyrum Smith at Carthage Jail. And out of this great tragedy, Jason again finds and strengthens his testimony. Jason often steps out of the action to talk to the audience.

<u>MONOLOGUE: 1M(teen) • JASON -- Scene One</u>
ABOUT THE CHARACTER:
JASON: *is the 14 year old subject of the play. A youth whose father was killed in Missouri and who sees the Saints suffering in Nauvoo and then witnesses the Prophet Joseph being shot by a mob. This monolog happens right after the Mob comes to his farm and threatens him and his family, but before the Martyrdom.*

JASON: I never forgot that moment -- that very moment of denial, betrayal. That's how I looked at it years later. I never forgot the pain and humiliation either. You can't imagine what it's like or how it feels for the cold dirty steel of a bunch of misfits to pierce into your flesh on every side. I was hot-cold-hot again. And not only hot with pain, I was hot with anger. And my anger wasn't at these devil's agents. I was angry at the God who was making me suffer the pain. The God who held my tongue while my blood ran down the outside of my skin. The God who held me like a steel trap while I suffered at the hands of my enemies. That's what I thought -- then. I have never nor will I ever forget my thoughts and words of that terrible moment. "I ain't no Mormon -- just leave me alone!"

Zion BookWorks

They Called Him Brother Joseph
A Musical by *Elizabeth Hansen* and *C. Michael Perry*

ABOUT THE PLAY: It is 1855. Lucy Mack Smith is near death and has compiled her memoirs into a biography of her son, Joseph Smith -- The Prophet. She has a young visitor who is interviewing her for the newspaper and asking her all about that "ol' Joe Smith". She says his name was Joseph -- but they all called him Brother Joseph. She takes us through bits and pieces of the Prophet's life in a celebration of the man and his relationship to God, his family, his friends, his congregations and even his enemies -- where we find that he was always "Brother Joseph". All the characters are seen through the eyes of the mother of a Prophet of God.

<u>MUSICAL SCENE: 1M 1W • JOSEPH Smith & EMMA Smith -- Act 1</u> *(This is a musical scene where the dialog and the song cannot be separated.)*
ABOUT THE CHARACTERS:
JOSEPH: The boy Prophet, the Restorer, the imperfect man who longs for the perfection and the approval of his God. He is dedicated to the promulgation of the Gospel of his Savior, Jesus Christ. But he also enjoys his simple humanity, a gift from God.
EMMA: loves Joseph fiercely and Like any young woman sees herself with him forever. She is pleased with how things are progressing, but cautious because of her father.

MUSICAL # 7 -- EVERYTHING AND MORE

EMMA:
    JOSEPH... JOSEPH...

JOSEPH: Since Alvin died I have been more lonely that a man ever could or ever should be.
> *(A LIGHT rises on EMMA, a lovely young woman of 20.)*

EMMA:
>PAPA SAYS HE LIKES YOU.
>I ALWAYS KNEW HE WOULD.
>MAMA HAS HER DOUBTS.
>BUT I THINK YOU SHOULD...

JOSEPH: I have been giving this much thought...

EMMA:
>TELL HER HOW YOU'LL GIVE ME
>EVERYTHING AND MORE.
>AND YOU'LL MAKE ME SMILE
>LIKE I'VE NEVER SMILED BEFORE.

JOSEPH: Miss Emma Hale is not like any other woman I have ever seen.
>SHE'S EVERYTHING I WANT AND MORE.

EMMA: Papa... Mama...

JOSEPH:
>MOTHER SAYS SHE LIKES YOU,
>I DIDN'T THINK SHE WOULD.
>FATHER HAS HIS DOUBTS
>ABOUT MY LIVELIHOOD.

EMMA: Joseph has asked me to— —
> *(She stops and listens to her unseen mother.)*

Joseph...Smith.

JOSEPH:
>I WILL TELL HER FATHER
>THAT I WILL ADORE
>HER. THE DREAMS SHE DREAMS
>WILL BECOME OUR DREAMS AND MORE.

EMMA: No, Mama, Joseph Smith. You know very well who I'm talking about, Mama.
> *(SMITH, SR., exits but LUCY remains and watches JOSEPH and EMMA. Her light dims but doesn't go out.)*

>HE'S EVERYTHING I WANT AND MORE.

JOSEPH:
>A CASTLE ON A HILL,
>AND DRESSES OF BROCADE.
>SERVANTS TO ATTEND YOU,
>THAT'S HOW DREAMS ARE MADE.

EMMA:
>A BUSINESS THAT IS BOOMING
>AND LOUNGING IN THE SHADE.
>STABLES FULL OF HORSES,
>THAT'S HOW DREAMS ARE MADE.

JOSEPH: Lounging in the shade. I haven't had enough of that.
>*(They come together CENTER and take hands.)*

EMMA: Dresses of brocade. It is a lovely thought, isn't it?
>*(He nods.)*

But I've heard brocade is heavy...and uncomfortable.

JOSEPH: And I've never been one to lounge.

EMMA:
>A DRESS OF PLAIN DESIGN, IN GRAY OR GREEN OR BLUE,
>WITHOUT RIPS OR TEARS,
>JUST A DRESS THAT WEARS,
>WOULD BE EVERYTHING, IT'S TRUE.

JOSEPH:
>A FARM WITH LIVESTOCK AND A BARN THAT HAS A DOOR.
>WHERE, THROUGH THICK AND THIN,
>ALL THE CROPS COME IN,
>WOULD BE EVERYTHING AND MORE.

BOTH:
>DREAMS ARE SOON FORGOTTEN,
>NOT FORGOTTEN, JUST REPLACED.
>WITH THE SIMPLE HOPE OF LIFE
>WHERE HARDSHIPS CAN BE FACED.
>IF WE ARE TOGETHER, YES,
>TOGETHER NOT ALONE,
>NO POWER CAN UPSET US,
>WITH THE WINDS WE'LL NOT BE BLOWN.

JOSEPH:
>A PLACE TO LIVE AND BREATHE, WHERE LIFE IS NOT A CHORE.
>STEADY WORK IS NICE,
>SPRING WITHOUT THE ICE,
>WOULD BE EVERYTHING AND MORE.

EMMA:
>ONE SMALL CABIN, WITH A STURDY WOODEN FLOOR,
>WINDOWS FRAMED IN LACE,
>AND WITH GLASS IN PLACE,
>WOULD BE EVERYTHING AND MORE.

BOTH:
>A FAMILY OF OUR OWN, WITH CHILDREN BY THE SCORE.
>WARM AND COLD WITH YOU.
>GROWING OLD WITH YOU,
>WOULD BE EVERYTHING AND MORE.
>
>GROWING OLD WITH YOU,
>WARM AND COLD WITH YOU,
>YEARS UNTOLD WITH YOU,
>WOULD BE EVERYTHING AND MORE.

The sheet music to this scene is available from the publisher for $1.00 in a PDF file.

MUSICAL SCENE: 2M(1teen) • *JOSEPH Smith & ALVIN Smith -- Act 1* (A musical scene where the song and dialog are inseparable)
ABOUT THE CHARACTERS:
JOSEPH: At age 14 he witnessed a Holy Vision of God The Father and God The Son. He could in no way deny it. He was not unlike any young man of any time period -- testing, trying, hoping, praying -- and he had a family given to him by God, so that he could create a great work for the

Children of Men.
ALVIN: *Joseph's ever-encouraging eldest brother. Alvin died before the Church was organized. But they were closer than brothers around the time of the First Vision. This is Alvin's pre-conversion story, where he sees the divine mission of his younger sibling through Joseph's recounting of The First Vision.*

> *(Lights up on the YOUNG JOSEPH AND ALVIN tableau.)*

ALVIN: Yes, you are.

YOUNG JOSEPH: No, I ain't. It's the truth, Alvin. You can bust my head wide open, let my brains fall right on the ground, but it won't make it be any less true.
> *(ALVIN releases him and raises a warning finger.)*

ALVIN: This is important, Joseph. If yer lyin' to me I <u>will</u> bust your head.

YOUNG JOSEPH: If I'm lyin' God'll bust my head. But I ain't lyin', Alvin, honest.
> *(ALVIN walks a few steps away, thinking, then turns.)*

ALVIN: It's just so hard to believe.
> *(ALVIN thrusts his hands in his pockets and thinks. HE makes several false starts, then SINGS. MUSIC STARTS.)*

MUSICAL # 6 -- WHAT WAS IT LIKE?

ALVIN:
> SO, WHAT WAS IT LIKE?
> WHEN HE SHOWED HISSELF TO YOU.
> MOST OF US ARE UNFIT LIKE
> FER THE ALMIGHTY TO TALK TO.
>
> WAS HE BIG AS THE SKY?
> AND HOW DID HE SPEAK?
> IN A THUNDEROUS CRY?

OR MILDLY, MYSTERIOUS AND MEEK?
(YOUNG JOSEPH shakes his head.)

YOUNG JOSEPH:
YOU GOT IT ALL WRONG,
LIKE OTHERS BEFORE,
HE SPOKE LIKE A MAN WITH A MOUTH,
NOTHIN' MORE.

HE ISN'T A CLOUD 'ER A TEMPEST, 'ER SUCH
AND I SAW, AS I BOWED,
A MAN I COULD TOUCH.

BOTH:
A VISION OF GOD,
NOT SINCE MOSES OF OLD,
NOT SINCE PAUL STOOD SO AWED,
WAS A MAN SO CONSOLED.

ALVIN:
BUT YOU'RE JUST A BOY
AND HE SPOKE TO YOU.

YOUNG JOSEPH:
THAT'S TRUE I'M A BOY
WASN'T DAVID ONE TOO?
And Samuel.

ALVIN:
WHAT DOES IT ALL MEAN, DO YOU THINK?
WHAT'S HE TRYING TO SAY TO US ALL?
WHAT DO WE GLEAN, DO YOU THINK?
WE ARE HUMANS SO WEAK AND SMALL.

YOUNG JOSEPH:
IT MEANS GOD IS STILL HERE
AND HE WANTS US TO KNOW,
HE'LL RETURN TO US SOON,
'CUZ HE LOVES US ALL SO.

AND MERE WORDS CAN NOT TELL
HOW HIS VOICE LIKE A SPIKE
PIERCED MY SOUL...
THAT'S WHAT IT WAS LIKE.

BOTH:
>THIS VISION OF GOD,
>NOT SINCE MOSES OF OLD,
>NOT SINCE PAUL STOOD SO AWED,
>WAS A MAN SO CONSOLED.

YOUNG JOSEPH:
>THOUGH I'M JUST A BOY,
>I KNOW HOW IT SOUNDS.
>I FELT GOD'S JOY.
>IT WAS PROFOUND.

BOTH:
>WHAT'S HAPPENIN' HERE, DO YOU THINK?
>WHAT DOES GOD HAVE IN STORE?
>WHEN EVER'THING'S CLEAR, DO YOU THINK...
>GOD WILL SAY MORE?

The sheet music to this scene is available from the publisher for $1.00 in a PDF file.

The Unfortunate Courtship of Brian Tanner
A Short Play By *Jerry Argetsinger*

ABOUT THE PLAY:

<u>COMIC: 2M • BRIAN & MATT -- Scene One</u>
ABOUT THE CHARACTERS:
BRIAN: the perpetual bachelor -- in Frontier Utah of all places! Only in his mid-to-late 20s, he just hasn't found 'the right one'. He's looked, but life somehow got in the way
MATT: also in his mid-20s, and a bachelor and BRIAN's close friend.

BRIAN: *(Miserable.)* Wonderful. We'll be happy to help. Matt, do you think...
  (Matt breaks out laughing, making Brian mad.)
All right!
MATT: I'm sorry. But you should have seen the look on your face.
BRIAN: Traitor!
MATT: You know I'm on your side. You just don't see the humor in the situation.
BRIAN: That's right. I do fail to see the humor in this situation. How would you like it if everyone in the world teamed up against you?
MATT: It's not that bad. They weren't that bad looking either.
BRIAN: They weren't bad looking, were they! Did you get a good look at Cheryl?
MATT: Does the sun shine?
BRIAN: With her around I don't think you'd notice.
MATT: *(Teasing.)* You're not interested, are you?
BRIAN: Don't worry! I will not fall for one of my aunt's schemes.
MATT: Then what are you going to do?

BRIAN: Aunt May has to think that I'm trying to find a wife or she won't get off my back.

MATT: How are you going to make her think you are when you aren't?

BRIAN: I know! I'll pretend to be interested in one of the girls. Then, when it's time for them to go on to Arizona I'll just tell Aunt May that it didn't work out. Then I'll be back where I started... a free man!

MATT: What happens if the woman you pretend to be interested in falls madly in love with you?

BRIAN: I won't give them any ideas. I'll just let Aunt May think that I'm trying.

MATT: I'm not so sure it'll work. Salt Lake women only go to Arizona for one reason.

BRIAN: I know. To get married. There aren't enough men in Salt Lake.

MATT: That's right. So you know what they're after.

BRIAN: Maybe I could propose to all of them. That should fix their wagon until they get their wagon fixed.

MATT: What do you do if they accept?

BRIAN: If I can make myself obnoxious enough, they won't accept.

MATT: Out of three women, at least one will accept. What happens if more than one accepts? You can't handle one, let alone two or three.

BRIAN: Look who's talking! It wasn't me that had to go home last Saturday night and leave my date. I entertained my date and yours with no problem.

MATT: That's different. I got sick.

BRIAN: Oh yeah... "Awkward-i-tis!"

MATT: Back to the point. What are you going to do if any of them accept your gallant proposal?

BRIAN: I'll just play them off against each other.

MATT: That might just work. But... how are you going to propose?

BRIAN: One at a time.

MATT: I think you should ask the whole bunch at once.

BRIAN: And we can invite the neighbors in, too.

MATT: Think about it, Brian. Three desperate, man-hungry women, each thinking that she is the one and only...

BRIAN: I see your point.

MATT: You'd better put a lot of thought into this, Romeo.

BRIAN: Why don't you go home?

MATT: As a matter of fact, I do have to help Charley close up the livery stable. Good luck! You're going to need it.

BRIAN: Why don't you come around after supper. You could take one of them off my hands.

MATT: What would my girl think!

BRIAN: If you explain that you're going for sparking lessons, she'll drag you here!

(Matt grabs a handful of beans and throws them at Brian who laughs and chases him out of the store.)

Zion BookWorks

Wisdom Tree
A Musical By *Max C. Golightly*, *Yutonna Kerbs* and others

ABOUT THE PLAY: The story of White Settlers contracted by the US Government to settle near a Ute Indian Reservation in Southern Utah in 1852. As the two groups learn to work and live together there are trials and almost even disaster. But the young people of the two cultures find a way to bring about peace in what could have been a troubled world. The wisdom in the story comes from the Native American tradition of the wise old tree, and supplication to the spirit of that tree, as well as to the Great Spirit, to solve problems.

DRAMATIC SCENE: 1M 1W (both teens) • PENEWAH & WILLKIE -- Act 1 *(the language is not meant in a comic vein, nor meant to demean. The Native American tongues did not incorporate the use of 'articles', it was strange to them, like most of the ways of the invading Europeans.)*
ABOUT THE CHARACTERS:
PENEWAH: *the daughter of the Indian Chief, is bound to another of her tribe, but her heart has been won by this strange White Boy. She has taken him to see the Wisdom Tree, a sacred spot for her people.*
WILLKIE: *Has fallen head over heels in love with the beautiful daughter of the Chief of the local Ute tribe. He is always trying to teacher her the ways of his people, while hoping to learn the ways of hers.*

PENEWAH: Here I am, Willkie.
WILLKIE: *(Holding head)* So this is Wisdom Tree!
PENEWAH: We come here when we are sad and when we are happy.
WILLKIE: What can it do for a headache? Wow!
PENEWAH: Willkie not feel well?
WILLKIE: Willkie have big warpath in head. Willkie not drink hard cider again.

PENEWAH: Penewah not drink again. When all was smiles on faces of my people, we choose such a tree in other fields, wherever we go. We sit in shade in summer and in moontime. We wish for things our heart wants and sometimes these things happen. We always find wisdom under tree.

WILLKIE: So, this is your Wisdom Tree?

PENEWAH: Yes, her roots are deep in soil; her branches pray to sky. Man or Woman whose arms reach high to Great Spirit will have new strength -- strength of tree, Tree listens.

WILLKIE: It does? I ... I have brought you something,
(Hands her a small box which she ponders over.)
Gifts.

PENEWAH: Gifts?

WILLKIE: Something someone gives to someone to please them,

PENEWAH: Like small bird or colored stone!

WILLKIE: You're supposed to open it up. Like this.

PENEWAH: Aiyee! It is handsome!

WILLKIE: Candy! Taste it!

PENEWAH: I have candy before. I am pleased!
(Tastes candy.)

WILLKIE: Came all the way from New Orleans. I have, something else.
(Hands her buckle)

PENEWAH: You give this to me also?
(Discovering the reflection of the moon in the buckle.)
Aiyee! The moon is smiling at us!
(HE looks and they discover each other.)
I so happy, Willkie.

WILLKIE: Not in your hair. Here.
(Puts it around her neck.)

PENEWAH: Willkie not like Penewah's hair?

WILLKIE: Very much!

PENEWAH: You want to kiss Penewah?

WILLKIE: Yes, but ...

PENEWAH: Tendranee say that is white man's way after giving present. Tendranee is best friend, Squandro's sister.

WILLKIE: Squandro?

PENEWAH: Squandro has pleasant voice, pleasant face.

WILLKIE: Handsome?

PENEWAH: Handsome! He wants Penewah.

WILLKIE: How do you know'?

PENEWAH: Squandro gives Penewah presents, too. Small birds, pretty birds stuffed with prairie grass. He brings rabbit skins and stones with colored faces; I sew them in his moccasins. I am good skin-maker.

(Pause)

You want to kiss Penewah, now?

WILLKIE: We ... like to lead up to that sort of thing.

PENEWAH: Ahyee! Like leading horse to water?

WILLKIE: Kind of like that -- yeah!

(WILKIE kisses PENEWAH on the cheek.)

PENEWAH: Why do you do that?

WILLKIE: That is kiss. I mean, that is a kiss.

PENEWAH: Not the same kiss Tendranee tell about.

WILLKIE: When a man likes a woman, he first leads up ... by putting an arm around her ... like this.

PENEWAH: Protect her from rain and snow?

WILLKIE: That's it! Then, he kisses her.

(WILKIE Kisses her on the lips. SHE stars blankly, then steps forward, turns him around, puts her arms firmly around his neck and kisses him long and hard and then looks u-p with a please expression.)

PENEWAH: Penewah like kiss!

(Kisses him again.)

Kissing strangely warm; makes fever! Penewah like kiss!

(Kisses him again. HE backs up, incredulous.)

WILLKIE: Whew! Moonlight has a strange effect on Indians, doesn't it?

(Some birdcalls at a distance.)

PENEWAH: *(Alarmed)* Squandro comes. You must go!

WILLKIE: I'm not afraid of Squandro!

PENEWAH: He will kill you!

WILLKIE: Squandro isn't going to kill anyone!

PENEWAH: You make promise you go away when Penewah say. You go now!

(Birdcalls again, nearer.)

WILLKIE: Will you meet me again -- tomorrow.

PENEWAH: Yes, go now!

(WILLKIE goes, returning immediately.)

WILLKIE: I just wanted to tell you that you are really something.
   (Disappears)
PENEWAH: *(Starting after him, touching her lips)* Something -- Penewah is something.

DRAMATIC SCENE: 1M 1W • VENICE & DENVER -- Act 2
ABOUT THE CHARACTERS:
VENICE: She tended DENVER and nursed him and kind of fell in love with him, despite the fact that she had a husband, Guylan, at the time, who has now left her. She is starting over.
DENVER: was found by the people of this settlement alongside the road, a victim of amnesia. Only called Denver because that's where he remembers coming from, until just before this scene. He and Venice have grown close.

VENICE: *(Breathless)* They told me at the store, you know who you are!
DENVER: *(Striking pose)* Joshua Keeley, landowner, dealer in men's clothing! It seems I disappeared from Denver about seven months ago. Or so Gil Powers says!
VENICE: Always knew you were someone ... important.
DENVER: Did you?
VENICE: *(With some difficulty)* Just my luck. You teach me to say 'Au Revoir' in French and then make it necessary to use it!
   (They exchange a look)
   You have to go so soon?
DENVER: The snows begin in October, Venice and Mrs. Daley wants to be with her son. And I've been Mr. Nobody much too long.
VENICE: These last four months have filled a lifetime. I ... get panicky thinking about your not being here -- our not studying together.
DENVER: You know enough to keep on by yourself.
VENICE: It still won't be the same ...
   (Desperately)

He's gone, Denver. Guylan's gone. He left yesterday afternoon and didn't come home last night. Since Marga married Avaronche, he's been -- detached, as if he wasn't certain about anything. He looks at me whenever I talk about Marga as if I were responsible for that.

DENVER: But Marga's been very happy ...

VENICE: Oh, yes! A different woman -- singing, and ... fulfilled.

DENVER: Venice, Guylan came by yesterday to talk with me -- about us.

VENICE: What did you tell him?

DENVER: The truth. That I love you and if there's any possibility that you're not going to make it together, I wanted you to go with me -- to Salt Lake and to Colorado.

VENICE: He didn't think ... didn't accuse us of anything, did he?

DENVER: He loves you, Venice. As much as I do.

VENICE: He doesn't ever say he does.

DENVER: When he left here, I was worried about him, so I asked him where he was going. 'Out to f ind myself,' he said. He's at the hogan with Marga.

VENICE: Does he mean to find himself out there?

DENVER: I've watched you both when you're together. That something that brought you together is still there -- under the words you haven't said, the joys you haven't experienced. He loves you, but he doesn't know how to say it after all these years.

VENICE: You talk as if you know what its all about.

DENVER: I don't know that I do, but I do know your husband is looking for a way to bring it all back --- the magic of that love you've lost.

VENICE: Thats beautiful, Denver. It belongs in a story.

(Pause.)

What you said a moment ago -- about lovin' me? Do you mean that?

DENVER: Don't you know that I do?

VENICE: Well, I suppose the kind of ... thing we've enjoyed -- our talks over my lessons and all, that doesn't happen with just anyone.

(SHE reaches out her hand to HIM, which he takes.)

I want so much to go with you, leave all this behind.

DENVER: He's coming back this evening. He knows I leave tomorrow morning. If you can't find each other, come with me.
(SHE hugs him.)
VENICE: You are a joy no matter who you are or where you came form, but it isn't that simple between Guylan and me. I need to be certain, before I go, that those vows we made to each other don't mean anything.
DENVER: You don't want me anymore -- in the case that they don't?
VENICE: *(Kissing him on the cheek)* I'll see you in the morning -- no matter what.

<u>SERIO-COMIC SCENE (with optional song): 2M (1 a boy) •
MATT & JAY -- Act 2</u>
ABOUT THE CHARACTERS:
MATT: is a father, a writer struggling to create the play that is happening all around him; a play that his son believes in and wants to see done. A play about their ancestors and their interactions with the Ute Indian Tribe of Utah.
JAY: is the son, around 11 or 12. He loves his father and misses his dead mother. They have both been somewhat solitary since his mother's death and this scene is one of the first of their reconnection.

The attic stairway of the Keeley home. JAY is hiding in the stairway. MATT pulls imaginary gun, shoots. JAY shoots. MATT falls dead on the couch.
MATT: *(LAUGHING)* What an easy way to die!
JAY: Bad always dies easy!
MATT: Not lately.
(Pulling him down on couch, wrestling.)
Say! I haven't seen you much lately.
JAY: Grammaw says I shouldn't come up when you're writing. But, I snuck up yesterday -- when you were gone.
MATT: And?
JAY: *(Picking up a journal)* I ... I read this journal.
MATT: And?

JAY: Was what GreatGrandpa wrote about in his diary really true?

MATT: 'Fraid so.

JAY: I don't know what I would do -- if something happened to you.

MATT: You've got Grammaw.

JAY: Yeah -- and I love her -- but she's not you.

MATT: *(Seeing book in JAY's hand)* What's that?

JAY: Grandpa's journal. There's some great stuff in here.

MATT: Really? You really read it?

JAY: Yeah. Why? Shouldn't I have?

MATT: I just never thought you'd be interested.

JAY: I love it, Dad!

MATT: Wanna have a sleepover? We'll read it again -- together.

JAY: Grammaw said not to bother you.
  (Whispers)
  When?

MATT: How about tonight?

JAY: *(Rushes to MATT's arms)* I love it up here, Dad!
  (JAY is at window)
  You can see wider than the whole sky! There must be a million stars!

MATT: More than a million!

JAY: How big would you say the sky is, Dad?

MATT: Hard to say.
  (MATT joins JAY at the window.)

MUSICAL #13 -- IF YOUR HEART'S IN IT!

MATT:
  A THING IS AS BIG AS YOU WANT IT TO BE,
  AS GOOD OR AS BAD AS YOU FIND IT.
  A THING'S ONLY SMALL IF YOU LET IT BE SMALL
  A CLOCK ONLY TICKS IF YOU WIND IT.
  THE SKY IS AS BIG AS YOU WANT IT TO BE.
  AS HIGH AND AS WIDE AS THE EYE CAN SEE.
  YOU CAN SOAR, YOU CAN SAIL,
  YOU CAN FLY WITHOUT FAIL,
  OVER EVERY DETAIL OF THIS WORLD
  IF YOUR HEART'S IN IT.

BOTH:
YOU CAN SOAR, YOU CAN SAIL,
YOU CAN FLY WITHOUT FAIL,
OVER EVERY DETAIL OF THIS WORLD
IF YOUR HEART'S IN IT.

The sheet music is available from the Publisher for $1.00 in PDF format.

COPYRIGHTS AND PERMISSIONS

The rights granted by the inclusion of the excerpted works in this book are severely limited. All scenes, songs and monologs may be used in classroom situations, and any performance showcases resulting from that classwork; they may also be used as audition material by any actor in any situation in order to secure a role (or a call-back); they may NOT be used without a slight charge as part of an evening's entertainment, whether or not for profit, that does not result from a class, workshop or seminar.

- **And Some Cried Fraud!** -- A Play by *Thom Duncan*. © 1998 by *MarvelousWorks*. ALL RIGHTS RESERVED. Public performance rights and licensing held by Zion Theatricals (www.ziontheatricals.com)
- **The Anointed** -- A Musical by *Thomas F. Rogers and C. Michael Perry*. © 1980, 1983 & 2013 by *Thomas F. Rogers and C. Michael Perry*. ALL RIGHTS RESERVED. Public performance rights and licensing held by Zion Theatricals (www.ziontheatricals.com)
- **Brothers** -- A Play by *J. Scott Bronson*. © 2010 by *J. Scott Bronson*. ALL RIGHTS RESERVED. Public performance rights and licensing held by Zion Theatricals (www.ziontheatricals.com)
- **The Brothers** -- A Play by *Christie Lund Coles*. © 1966 by *Christie Lund Coles*. ALL RIGHTS RESERVED. Public performance rights and licensing held by Zion Theatricals (www.ziontheatricals.com)
- **Charlie's Monument** -- a Musical by *Susan McCloud, Marvin Payne and K. Newell Dayley* © 1987 by *Marvin Payne* & © 1982 by *Kanada Music*. ALL RIGHTS RESERVED. Public performance rights and licensing held by Zion Theatricals (www.ziontheatricals.com)
- **The Dance** -- A Musical by *Carol Lynn Pearson & J.A.C. Redford*. © 1983 by *Carol Lynn Pearson and J.A.C. Redford*. ALL RIGHTS RESERVED. Public performance rights and licensing held by Zion Theatricals (www.ziontheatricals.com)
- **Family** -- A Play by *Eric Samuelsen*. © 2003 by *Eric Samuelsen*. ALL RIGHTS RESERVED. Public performance rights and licensing held by Zion Theatricals (www.ziontheatricals.com)
- **Fire In The Bones** -- A Play by *Thomas F. Rogers*. © 1976 by *Thomas F. Rogers*. ALL RIGHTS RESERVED. Public performance rights and licensing held by Zion Theatricals (www.ziontheatricals.com)
- **The Forge and the Fire** -- A Musical By *Max C. Golightly*, and

others. © 1975 by Max C. Golightly. ALL RIGHTS RESERVED. Public performance rights and licensing held by Zion Theatricals (www.ziontheatricals.com)

Huebener -- A Play by *Thomas F. Rogers.* © 1976 & 1992 by Thomas F. Rogers. ALL RIGHTS RESERVED. Public performance rights and licensing held by Zion Theatricals (www.ziontheatricals.com)

Jedediah! -- A Musical by *James G. Lambert* and *C. Michael Perry.* © 1997 by James G. Lambert and C. Michael Perry. ALL RIGHTS RESERVED. Public performance rights and licensing held by Zion Theatricals (www.ziontheatricals.com)

Liberty Jail -- A Musical by *Orson Scott Card* and *C. Michael Perry.* © 1978 by Orson Scott Card & C. Michael Perry. ALL RIGHTS RESERVED. Public performance rights and licensing held by Zion Theatricals (www.ziontheatricals.com)

Martyr In Waiting -- a short play by *Carol Lynn Pearson.* © 1968 by Carol Lynn Pearson. ALL RIGHTS RESERVED. Public performance rights and licensing held by Zion Theatricals (www.ziontheatricals.com)

Matters of the Heart -- A Play by *Thom Duncan.* © 1985 & 1997 by MarvelousWorks. ALL RIGHTS RESERVED. Public performance rights and licensing held by Zion Theatricals (www.ziontheatricals.com)

Move On! -- A Play *by Carol Lynn Pearson.* © 1974 by Carol Lynn Pearson. ALL RIGHTS RESERVED. Public performance rights and licensing held by Zion Theatricals (www.ziontheatricals.com)

The Plan -- a Play by *Eric Samuelsen.* © 2007 by Eric Samuelsen. ALL RIGHTS RESERVED. Public performance rights and licensing held by Zion Theatricals (www.ziontheatricals.com)

The Planemaker -- A musical play by *Marvin Payne and Guy Randle.* © 1983 by Marvin Payne & Guy Randle. ALL RIGHTS RESERVED. Public performance rights and licensing held by Zion Theatricals (www.ziontheatricals.com)

Reunion -- A Play by *Thomas F. Rogers.* © 1980 by Thomas F. Rogers. ALL RIGHTS RESERVED. Public performance rights and licensing held by Zion Theatricals (www.ziontheatricals.com)

A Sceptre, A Sword, A Scented Rose -- A Play by *Thom Duncan.* © 1980 by MarvelousWorks. ALL RIGHTS RESERVED. Public performance rights and licensing held by Zion Theatricals (www.ziontheatricals.com)

Stones -- A Play by *J. Scott Bronson.* © 2002 by J. Scott Bronson. ALL RIGHTS RESERVED. Public performance rights and licensing held by Zion Theatricals (www.ziontheatricals.com)

A Teenage Witness To The Martyrdom -- A Short Musical by *C. Michael Perry.* © 1984 by C. Michael Perry. ALL RIGHTS RESERVED. Public performance rights and licensing held by Zion Theatricals (www.ziontheatricals.com)

They Called Him Brother Joseph -- A Musical by *Elizabeth Hansen* and *C. Michael Perry*. © *2005 by Elizabeth Hansen & C. Michael Perry. ALL RIGHTS RESERVED. Public performance rights and licensing held by Zion Theatricals (www.ziontheatricals.com)*

The Unfortunate Courtship of Brian Tanner -- a short play by *Jerry Argetsinger.* © *1976 & 1997 by Jerry Argetsinger. ALL RIGHTS RESERVED. Public performance rights and licensing held by Zion Theatricals (www.ziontheatricals.com)*

Wisdom Tree -- A Musical By *Max C. Golightly*, *Yutonna Kerbs* and others. © *1970 & 2012 by Max C. Golightly & C. Michael Perry. ALL RIGHTS RESERVED. Public performance rights and licensing held by Zion Theatricals (www.ziontheatricals.com)*

NOTE: If you choose to purchase one or any of the songs that go with the musical scenes, your $1.00 purchase entitles you to perform the scene or monolog in classes or at auditions, but not at public performances. It also authorizes you to make photocopies, or prints from your computer for yourself and your accompanist only. You cannot distribute this material to anyone else. Thank you.

RESOURCES

ACTING by Richard Boleslavsky -- Theatre Arts, Inc. -- 1934

ACTING IN FILM by Michael Caine -- Applause Books, 1997 -- ISBN: 1-55783-277-3

ACTING PROFESSIONALLY by Robert Cohen -- Barnes & Noble, 1972

AUDITION by Michael Shurtleff -- Walker, 1978 -- ISBN: 0-8027-7240-4

AUDITIONING FOR THE MUSICAL THEATRE by Fred Silver -- Newmarket Press, 1985

GOD'S FOOLS -- Plays of Mitigated Conscience by Thomas F. Rogers -- Signature Books, 1983

HUEBENER and Other Plays by Thomas F. Rogers -- Poor Robert's Publications, 1992 -- ISBN: 0-9632618-0-0

SAINTS ON STAGE Mahonri Stewart (ed.) -- Zarahemla Books, 2013 -- ISBN: 978-0-9883233-1-5

THE STANISLAVSKI SYSTEM by Sonia Moore -- Viking Compass, 1965

You can find some of the best audition and Monolog/Scene helps in video form on YouTube.

Sanford Meisner - Theater's Best Kept Secret (Part 1 of 7)
http://www.youtube.com/watch?v=zNuFSrsYfpM

Sanford Meisner - Theater's Best Kept Secret (Part 2 of 7)
http://www.youtube.com/watch?v=fa7BtUiZ79Y

Sanford Meisner - Theater's Best Kept Secret (Part 3 of 7)
http://www.youtube.com/watch?v=jQLFGAbY6ac

Sanford Meisner - Theater's Best Kept Secret (Part 4 of 7)
http://www.youtube.com/watch?v=rpb3A-SMjLI

(His work with Frances Sternhagen at the end of part 5 and the beginning of part 6 is some of the most brilliant monolog technique ever proposed.)

Sanford Meisner - Theater's Best Kept Secret (Part 5 of 7)
(http://www.youtube.com/watch?v=wES47t2k7k0)

Sanford Meisner - Theater's Best Kept Secret (Part 6 of 7)
http://www.youtube.com/watch?v=r7IUj8fTSiA

Sanford Meisner - Theater's Best Kept Secret (Part 7 of 7)
http://www.youtube.com/watch?v=Kp4wqTFeLYc

Michael Caine -- Acting In Film -- Part 1
http://www.youtube.com/watch?v=Njs6ZNSoFC0

Michael Caine -- Acting In Film -- Part 2
http://www.youtube.com/watch?v=hfv4TKu6mrE

Michael Caine -- Acting In Film -- Part 3
http://www.youtube.com/watch?v=s3adUch8mTU

Michael Caine -- Acting In Film -- Part 4
http://www.youtube.com/watch?v=NpX7wP3vo5s

Michael Caine -- Acting In Film -- Part 5
http://www.youtube.com/watch?v=9SVNHvsR710

Michael Caine -- Acting In Film -- Part 6
http://www.youtube.com/watch?v=uoaZfzHHPW4

www.ingramcontent.com/pod-product-compliance
Lightning Source LLC
Chambersburg PA
CBHW031941070426
42450CB00005BA/241